FAIL FAST,
MOVE FASTER

HTTP://WWW.FAILFASTMOVEFASTER.COM

ALSO BY JOSEPH PALLY

THE THINKING THINGS

WWW.THETHINKINGTHINGS.COM

FAIL FAST, MOVE FASTER

JUST BEING CURIOUS

BY

JOSEPH PALLY

SILKRAYS PUBLISHING, TEXAS
UNITED STATES OF AMERICA.

Fail Fast, Move Faster

Just Being Curious

Illustrations by:
Aneesh, Das, Deepu, Jay, Karnan, Mahesh, Prasanth and Varun.

Silkrays books may be ordered through booksellers or by contacting:

Silkrays Publishing Corporation
www.silkrays.com
silkrays.publishing@gmail.com

This book is based mostly on real-life events. All the characters, names, incidents, or organizations, and dialogue in this book are used fictitiously.

ISBN: 978-0-9824326-3-1 (pbk)

Printed in the United States of America.
Silkrays Rev. Date: 07/01/2009

Dedicated to the:

Greedless, for success is always yours.

Fearless, for you make the world what it should be.

Selfless, for you make a world worth living in.

"Anyone who has never made a mistake has never tried anything new."

Albert Einstein
(Nobel Laureate, 1879-1955)

******

"All men make mistakes, but only wise men learn from their mistakes."

Winston Churchill
(British Prime Minister during WWII, 1874-1965)

******

Contents

CHAPTER 1
A TALE OF TWO CITIES

Six-thirty am.

The sky cracks open another day. Church bells ring through the air.

The air is cold, the coldest it gets in the tropical city of Cochin.

Cochin is an interesting city. Called the Queen of the Arabian Sea, it is a city of less than a million; it is green as far as the eye can see.

The blue Arabian Sea lies to the west and the land is segmented by the calm Vembanad Lake. Graceful Chinese fishing nets (*cheena vala*) dot the shore close to where the sea meets the lake.

Life starts here slowly and continues at a deliberately slow speed.

Ferry boats carry thousands from the islands to the mainland. Ships bring in goods from other nations.

1

Planes deliver passengers from faraway places. Buses shuttle men, women and children to work and school. Men dodge city traffic on scooters.

It is a slow-motion tableau playing out under bright sunlight or dark monsoons.

The rising sun shines on everyone with the same gleaming streams of light. In two hours everyone is where they should be.

******

Halfway around the world, life starts later.

In Houston, Texas, a different people wake up, climb into their cars, and arrive at work and school.

Life is slightly faster – interrupted only by rare occurrences of wild spinning tornadoes or tortuous winding hurricanes.

Two sides of the same world, but not much different, if you look deep enough.

Our world is flat. Flatter than thirty years ago.

******

CHAPTER 2
A NEW DAY

I remember the first day I went to catch my new school bus.

It was my first trip alone and I was headed to a new school, and new friends.

I was a lanky kid, a fifth-grader in a white shirt and navy blue shorts carrying a bag of books, pencils, pens, and erasers. In the side pocket of my bag was a tiffin carrier with food – rice and omelets. I was excited; it was going to be the first time I ate from a tiffin-box.

With a book in my hand – I was reading and running at the same time to catch my bus.

I never stopped reading, even when I had to run. It was an easy way to cut off the world and avoid looking at girls.

The bus looked very different from what I had expected; I almost missed it. I guess the driver recognized my uniform and that's why he stopped to pick me up.

The trip was exciting for me.

It was raining slightly and it was a mysterious ride through streets I had never seen before.

The hour-long trip ended at a new school nestled among hills and trees, prefixed by an imposing church building.

Priests in white ran the school. They were disciplined as hell.

******

The teacher, Mr. Thomas, introduced to us the proper ways to behave in class: Say, "Pardon me," if you do not understand something. If you have a question, raise your hand. Be nice to everyone. Respect your teachers... and the stronger bullies.

I loved my school. It was a completely different experience.

So many teachers tried to teach us.

Mr. Zacharias taught us algebra.

Mr. Elias made us memorize the solution to quadratic equations.

Mr. John scared the daylights out of us – teaching us Malayalam, our mother tongue, using a thick cane that he used to beat kids who made mistakes.

Mr. Krishnan and Mr. Manmohan tried so hard to teach us Hindi, the national language.

They all focused on discipline. Mistakes were paid with caning.

No one wanted us to make mistakes.

Mistakes were bad. People who made them ended up not getting jobs.

******

Then there were a few passionate teachers.

Like Mr. Venkataraman, who taught us math. The Pythagorus Theorem, with proofs.

Or Mr. Kunjunni, the chemistry teacher, who taught us that the Periodic Table of Elements was all that we needed to know to master Chemistry.

Or Mr. Mathews, who spoke and taught English and insisted that we respond back to him in a language spoken by people half-a-world away.

******

Yet, one teacher made all the difference.

Mr. Mampilly, very old then, taught us how to learn.

He insisted on explaining every word. He showed us the movement of the planets and the sun with umbrellas and torchlight. He explained the seasons, day and night, tides and eclipses, using cricket balls, dusters, chalk pieces and books.

Lack of tools was never an issue for him. He gave us a perspective that no amount of caning could have.

Good teachers teach. Great teachers inspire.

******

Overall, the messages were the same as they teach elsewhere in the world.

Do not do anything out of the ordinary.

Learn. Do not think.

Do well. Do things as expected.

Anything else will land you with the higher authorities. Low marks. Low grades. Lowly jobs, or none at all.

Obedience was considered a virtue and discipline was a requirement for success in life.

I grew up in a culture in which making a mistake was exactly that, a mistake.

A decade later, I was transplanted to another land where mistakes were viewed as an acceptable part of life.

Yet neither taught me how to handle them.

Neither showed the essence of mistakes.

This book is about mistakes and how to make them so that your successes are far more exceptional than you ever thought they would be.

This book is about failing fast and moving faster, a philosophy that achieves tremendous results.

******

CHAPTER 3
BOYZ R BOYZ

Growing up in Downtown Cochin was interesting.

Like other boys, I loved trucks and cars.

Once I dreamed that two trucks lived on the dining table and that both were alive.

They talked to each other, and they looked up as I walked in. Like Thomas, the train.

Imagination is the greatest gift. And dreams are your best hope.

******

I wanted to drive trucks.

My mother would send me to the grocery store and I would imagine that there was a truck outside our house.

I would imagine getting into that imaginary truck, starting it with all the accompanying sounds, shifting the gears, and gaining speed as the gears shifted.

First gear... second gear... third gear... and finally, I'd reach the cruising speed.

9

I never drove in fourth or fifth gear. I left that to the professionals.

Turning the imaginary steering wheel, negotiating turns on the streets, dodging imaginary and real cars, and overtaking many of them.

Beep… Beep… Hmmmm… I would go.

I would downshift before arriving at the grocery store and park my imaginary truck in a safe position.

I would stop the truck, accompanied with all its sounds.

I would get out of the imaginary truck and give the grocery list to the shopkeeper.

******

I found grocery stores intriguing.

Prabhakaran's Grocery Store had a particular smell, of rice, spices, tamarind, and kerosene. Of powders: red, yellow, white…

They would fill the orders, do the math, add the numbers, take my money, and give me change. They would pack my items in newspaper cones tied with strings of jute.

I, in turn, would pack it in my satchel and go back to my imaginary parked truck.

******

I'd start the engines, accompanied again by the sounds.

Shift gears. Move reverse. Move forward.

First gear… Second gear…Third… back to the streets, turns, curves, speed up, slow down, stop, go, and get back home in a few minutes.

Satchel on my back full of paper cones holding rice, salt, powders, and more.

I would stop the imaginary truck, turn it off with the correct sounds, unload the cargo and give the goods to my mom.

Create with your mind. Make with your hands.

******

I got 10 paisa for making these purchases, which I used to buy sweets – red peanut candy was my favorite. If I got 25 paisa, I could buy bubble gum and blow big bubbles. Or I could buy a plastic sticker of Ritchie Rich, Phantom, or Donald Duck.

Bubble gum came with small stickers, but larger stickers cost more.

I remember that many things came with free items.

Colgate brand toothpaste usually came with little tiny plastic animals, tiny dinosaurs, tigers, and lions – cute beyond imagination. Signal brand had multicolored toothpaste – white and red – a fascinating start for any day.

What brand to buy was decided by what free items I would get, not what was good for the family's teeth.

Product marketing has not changed much over the years. Sell the sizzle, not the steak.

******

It was one of those days that three of us third-grade students hatched a plan to rob a store.

We named ourselves third-grade dacoits.

Glory & Company was located just next to St. Teresa's Convent School and sold carpets, mats, mattresses and a stick with beautiful multicolored feathers on it.

Those multicolored feathered sticks hung in front of the store.

I still have no idea who bought them, or what their purpose was. I had seen them behind the backseat headrests of some cars, where they seemed to serve no earthly purpose at all.

Red, yellow, white and green feathers – some just red, and some just green.

It was about four pm and our classes had just been dismissed.

Students in the uniform of white shirts and black-checked red shorts swarmed the streets, which were filled with cars.

Three of us, still in uniform, walked to the store like we were looking at mattresses.

We sprang into action.

I quickly grabbed at one of the feathered sticks. Unfortunately, the feathered stick did not come off.

I pulled at some of the multi-colored feathers instead and I got some.

We made our escape quickly, running back to school.

I thought that if the police chased us, we could hop into the school church and escape.

I heard the shopkeeper's screams behind us.

I dodged many cars. And rickshaws. And people.

I ran across the street. Then suddenly, a *Fiat* car hit me. I fell to the ground with red feathers clutched in my hand.

The driver thought it was blood, at first.

I was unhurt. The car had just started moving when it hit me and I had actually been moving faster than the car.

As for the robbery, the loot was not interesting at all; the thrill was in picking the feathers and running back in a rush of adrenaline.

I reached the school and saw other students waiting for the school bus.

"I was hit by a car," I boasted. It was not normal to get hit by a car. Few people live to talk about it.

Everyone looked at me like I was so lucky.

But I knew after that I would not make a good robber. I needed another career path.

Stealing is not fun.

******

Polson was the fattest kid in class back then and so we assumed that he was the strongest.

Then came Dan, the new face in second grade. He was thinner than Polson.

We had secret boxing bouts in the back row during class that day.

Polson fought Dan.

Dan bit Polson's ear (much like Tyson, the world-champ, decades later). Dan socked Polson on the stomach.

Polson gave up the fight with blood streaming down his ears.

I was up next against Dan, the winner.

I got up and went to the imaginary ring. It's no fun going up against a champion, especially in fistfights.

I closed my eyes, and thinking I was done, socked Dan in the face and then landed one on his tummy. Dan was on the floor with bloodstains.

I won the fight.

I was respected from then on, though I avoided fistfights.

Do not underestimate yourself.

******

I collected matchbox covers, pretty colored ones with pictures of cows, camels, trees and cars.

I collected them from the streets, matchboxes that smokers threw away when they were done. When I got a matchbox cover that was rare I showed it off to other friends with similar collections.

Richer kids collected postal stamps and coins. They had relatives abroad who sent them letters with pretty stamps.

Later we could buy foreign stamps in stores; the prettiest ones came from Bhutan. We did not need to have relatives abroad anymore to get stamps.

Stickers were a reward for my work, for getting groceries. Or they were my tips for attending school, if I felt lazy and did not want to go.

Polson saw my collection of stickers and came up with a great business proposal.

It went like this: I should give Polson all the stickers I had along with all the new ones I would buy that year. On the last day of class, he would give me five big foot-long stickers of Ritchie Rich and a few others. It was much like futures contracts of today.

My stickers were small, not more than a half-inch in height. This was a great deal. Polson became a good friend of mine from then on.

The last day of class came and fourth grade was over. We had to change schools that year because only girls continued on at that school. We would never see our classmates again.

It was the last day of class. I had dreamed of five big foot-long stickers and was eager to see them.

Polson was nowhere to be seen. In fact, I did not see him for another twenty years. By then he had become a restaurant owner and had totally forgotten about stickers.

Not everyone is trustworthy.

******

CHAPTER 4
LESSONS ON
WHEELS

Learning to ride a bicycle is always a great life lesson.

My dad's bicycle was beautiful.

It had multicolored rings around the hub that went round and round when he rode the bike, a cute plastic seat with covers on the triangular bar frame, and a small three-inch seat in the front of the horizontal bar to carry a kid. Brake levers with red plastic tubes on them. A carrying frame over the rear wheel to carry goods or a bigger kid, if need be.

A steel-coated dynamo connected to the back wheel that powered the steel-coated lamp in the front. At night, you would switch the dynamo on. The faster you went, the brighter the lamp burned, and the faster you could ride.

******

There are four phases to learning to ride a bicycle when you are small.

During the first phase, you learn to push the bicycle with one foot on the pedal, making quarter turns, with the other foot on the ground – sort of like jumping along beside the bicycle. The biker and the bike roughly balance each other like ballet dancers.

When you become more confident, you take the second leap of faith. Take the second leg and cross it over through the frame to the other side and make quarter turns with both feet on both pedals. This was trickier - stopping required you to jump out. This was like ballet dancing too, with the biker being supported fully by the bike.

In the third phase you stood over the two pedals, over the frame this time, but not actually sitting on the seat. If you had to stop, you would slow down, landing one or both feet on the ground.

In the final phase you could ride like anybody else. On the seat, with both feet on the pedals.

I graduated from first phase to the second in three days. Second to third in a week. I was on phase three for another two weeks. I never could get myself into phase four, the final phase.

I was on the way to the market to get vegetables, meat and fish. It was ten am and I was riding my dad's bicycle using third phase technique – standing on the pedals over the frame. Life was peaceful.

Suddenly, the road narrowed.

A huge yellow truck was in my way, coming towards me. I noticed possibly a clearance of about a foot or two on the left of the truck. I noticed a big drain on the left of this thin clearance.

There was no way to go.

I could not stop. I could not go.

The huge truck was too close and too fast.

I closed my eyes, pedaled as fast as I could, sat on the bicycle seat, and went for the clearance.

I knew that if I made it through this, I would live.

And I did.

I had finally moved on to phase four, when faced with certain death or serious injury.

When faced with a serious situation or death, close your eyes and do your best. You will come out okay.

If not, you won't have to worry about it – your choices will be limited any way.

So when face to face with fate, do not worry, and just go for it. In most cases, you will learn to survive better.

******

Learning to ride a bicycle is only half the game. Life can be dangerous on wheels – even when someone else is riding the bicycle and you are just a passenger.

It was my uncle this time. He was taking me to the new Sunday school and I was sitting in the carry frame at the back, my uncle on the seat.

He was a daredevil rider and rode the bicycle fast. Way too fast.

So fast that I asked him to slow down, twice. He would not listen and kept on riding faster than ever before.

So I just got off of the bike.

I have no idea what happened next.

As soon as I got off, a massive force pulled me forward. I was running faster than my body would take me. I ran right into a wall and collapsed to the ground.

I should have remembered Newton's First Law.

My body was in motion, on a fast moving bike. If I had to step off of it, I would continue to travel at the same speed, unless acted upon by and external unbalanced force, in this case, like the wall.

There was blood and white bandage on my face when I walked into the Sunday class.

I had on my father's new Seiko watch – with a black dial and golden hands – borrowed just for the day. It had scratches on its glass face from my fall.

You must know basic physics before you ride on a bicycle, or any two-wheeler. Even if you are just a passenger.

******

I used to ride fast. There were still things I did not know.

For example, you need to slow down when it rains.

It was on one of those rainy monsoon days that I found a reason to stop suddenly. There was a woman dressed in red with two men on either side of her, walking ahead of my bike.

There was no way for me to pass them safely, so I had to stop.

My bike refused to stop.

The woman was like a target in the middle and the bike hit her from behind. She fell screaming, with me and the bike tossed to the ground.

She must have thought she was dead, that she had been hit by something more serious.

21

"How dare you hit my darling?" screamed the man on the left, possibly my victim's husband.

"He has not even hatched from his egg yet. Wild kid," shouted the man on the right, possibly the victim's unstable brother. Since he now had my neck within his hands, I withheld my comments.

Physics tells you that friction in the brakes decreases when they get wet.

******

Once I wanted to test out a new way to ride a bike.

I wanted to hold the handle bars differently from how others did.

What if I had my left hand on my right side handle bar, and right hand on the left side handle bar?

I was riding near the *Toddy* (liquor made from palm trees) shop, when I decided to test this idea.

It was a few seconds before I realized I was inside a big dirty drain, with the bicycle above me, its multicolored rings on the wheel still going round and round.

That time I had bandages on my nose, hands and legs – just about everywhere.

Physics is very counter-intuitive. Especially when your right hand does not know what the left hand is doing.

******

CHAPTER 5
GAMEZ

The school playground had one soccer field, two basketball fields and a cricket pitch in the middle. After lunch, kids formed teams to play one or the other.

I never played any of these ball games. I did not know the rules.

I never played the games because the ball, bat and other accessories for those games cost a lot of money.

Only the rich kids could afford to play. Or the kids who had parents who adored them so much as to spend hundreds of rupees to make them happy. Or the kids who had parents with kids that were lovable and obedient enough to spare the change.

My parents did not have kids who were adorable, lovable or obedient; hence I never learned the rules of the ball games.

I looked around to see what I could play.

I tried hide-and-seek. I hid in the hay behind the school – no one ever found me – but my whole body itched when I got out of the hay.

I tried catch-me-if-you-can. We would jump several feet over fences, thorn-bushes and ditches – so dangerously sometimes that I wonder how I managed not to break more bones during that time.

I hadn't found my game yet.

******

Then I found a group of kids behind the playground, playing a new game.

The game was called *kuttiyum-kolum*. The game of a *kutty* (short stick) and a *kol* (long stick). Some called it *Gilli-danda*.

It was a simple game. You needed no initial investment to play.

A stick was all you needed, and that you could just get from the school neighbor's fence. We would bend one of the trees and break it off. We then broke the branch into two pieces, a small one-foot one for *kutti*, and a longer two-foot one for *kol*.

With the *kol*, we scratched a small, v-shaped notch in the ground.

The *kutty* would be laid over this v-shaped notch. The *kol* would then be inserted to the notch. The game would start with the player using the *kol* to lift the *kutty* off the ground, to send it flying off, with a sudden jerk.

The scoring was simple. You would measure the distance from the point that the *kutty* landed to the v-notch where the game started, in terms of the lengths of the *kol*. The farther the *kutty* went, the more *kol* lengths that would be added to the score.

******

The rules of the game were as complex as cricket and it had some unusual and strange aspects.

Let me mention some of the rules, as the game is not well documented.

The count started with *Vill*, followed by *Sadha, Muri, Nazhi, Eytti, Arennku* and back to *Vill*. Every *Vill* was a point. Your total score was the number of *Vill's* you could score.

But the fun started here. The next action depended on the last step you had counted. Depending on the count, you had to use a different body part to hold the *kutty* before flipping with a jerk to be then hit with the *kol*.

If you had ended with a *Sadha*, the player had to hold the *kutty* on his raised left foot while standing on just the right foot. With a jerk, the *kutty* would be flipped into the air, to be then hit using the *kol*. This was the second toughest shot to take.

For *Muri*, you could hold the *kutty* on your left hand vertically and then release it before hitting it. This was the easiest shot to take.

For *Nazhi*, you needed to keep the *kutty* over your left fingers while holding the palm downwards, and all except the little and the index fingers folded, somewhat like the war sign of the UT Texas Team.

For *Eytti*, you needed to hold the *kutty* over your left hand elbow, while keeping the elbow folded horizontally.

For *Arennku*, you had to look up and hold the *kutty* across the left eye. This was possibly the toughest shot to take.

If you rounded your score with a *Vill*, then you could keep the *kutty* over the v-notch, then use the *kol* to kick it far.

The other players would throw the *kutty* back from where it had landed. The player could kick it back – scoring again by measuring how far the *kutty* had gone. If the *kutty* was caught mid-flight, the player was out. If the *kutty* landed closer than a *kol*-length from the v-notch, the player was out.

That was it.

******

I had found my game.

There was no upfront investment needed. No initial setup.

You just had to make a hole in the ground.

And get some ordinary kids to play with you.

The type of stick you used improved the quality of the game, much like tennis rackets.

If you used a strong pine-like stick, the *kutty* could go far. If you used a thick stick like tapioca, the flight and the range of the *kutty* would be lower. The *kutty* or the *kol* could then break easily.

I was good at this game.

I loved it more than cricket.

We held matches against the students from other classes and we won often.

27

The players had no protective gear whatsoever.

But this simple game was my most comfortable game.

I was good at something.

The game taught me a lot.

That life can be dangerous when you are playing with sharp projectiles.

Everyone has an innate ability to be good at something.

******

I have not seen this game played for so many years. Someday, I hope to form a team of folks who may want to play it again.

Maybe someday it will even become an Olympics sport, with fiberglass *kutty* and *kol*, all made in China.

******

CHAPTER 6
A LEAF IN THE RAIN

Rains came often to our school, mostly during monsoons. The heavier the rain, the more of the playground became invisible.

I would run into the rain, deeper into the playground to watch the rain water drain into the channels.

The laterite soil had a light red tinge to it and when it mixed with the rainwater, the water would become deep orange red by the time it hit the drain.

I would drop leaves into the water and watch them float. Down the drain, down the plain, into the drain, into the channel, gathering speed as they went.

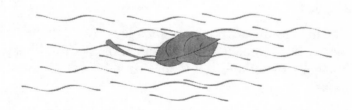

I would run after the leaves, chasing each of them, and finally bidding them good-bye as they were swept off into the larger drains.

I hoped the leaves had a nice trip downstream – into the Periyar River, then onto the Vembanad Lake, finally joining the Arabian Sea. Possibly even into the Indian Ocean.

I hoped that at least some of the leaves I sent would withstand the downstream journey. I imagined that a kid on some faraway beach might come across the leaves that I had sent.

I made paper ships with my name on them, and sent them to watch over the leaves.

Many of the paper ships would sink even before they reached the river.

Everything and everyone has a purpose. Not all achieve them.

******

The trees continued the rain, even after the skies had stopped.

The mango trees with green mangoes would swing in the wind, drenched in fresh rain. A few baby mangoes sometimes fell to the ground – a treat I often looked for.

But sometimes I wanted more than baby mangoes. I wanted real big green mangoes, directly off the tree.

I gathered some willing friends, and I gathered some rocks, and we pelted them at the bunch of mangoes up on a tree. The mangoes fell in twos and threes and we picked them up in our school bags.

Before long we saw the school peon walking toward us.

"The principal wants to see you," he said.

"Why?" I asked.

"He was watching you all from the window," he said. The principal's office was really far away, but he had a direct view of the mango tree that we had been pelting stones at.

Fr. Aaron did not cane us out of sheer mercy. Instead, he sent us back to the mango tree to stand under it for the rest of the day. We were to watch to make sure no one else pelted it.

Mercy teaches you more than beatings.

******

It was a few days later that I realized that laterite blocks could break if dropped from a height. The blocks had been kept for construction purposes, near the new school auditorium.

After another rain, I started lifting the laterite blocks and then dropping to watch them break into pieces.

This time Fr. Aaron sent me to Mr. John, the man with the big cane.

The caning was horrible, and I had to write an apology.

Break a few things. But learn fast.

******

While dropping the laterite blocks I had discovered a certain type of green moss. It had a capsule at the end of a stalk that carried spores.

My friends and I imagined the moss stalks were swords.

We devised a game where we picked a moss stalk each, interlocked the capsules and tried to pull the opponent's moss stalk. The one who could decapitate everyone else's moss stalk was the winner.

We ate the small black berries from the plants that grew nearby. They were sweet and we hoped were non-poisonous.

We made darts out of the top of a special type of grass, and threw them at the more gullible kids at school. We imagined we were American Indians, with poison darts, and that they were the gullible cowboys.

And we waited for the *touch-me-not* plants to open their leaves after the rain, and diligently poked each leaf to close them again.

Love nature.

******

They grew the best fruit trees inside the monastery – maybe on purpose. We would run to Fr. Silas, who always carried Rose Apples (*champakka*) he plucked from the trees inside.

When we had special retreats inside the monastery, we had a chance to see those trees. They had beautiful white flowers that looked like sunrays.

Fr. Pullepally lived inside the monastery.

He would get us the *Snehasena* (the army of love), a book that cost just 10 paisa and was filled with beautiful stories of love, charity and character. The book came with color drawings of great detail.

Fr. Pullepally also sold us books from faraway lands. They were slightly more expensive, but contained pictures that looked like Michelangelo had drawn them.

All the books talked about giving and selfless love and spread the word about the uselessness of greed, evil and selfishness.

The world outside was not so perfect. But the books showed us a world where love was perfect.

I was raised a Catholic – but I rebelled against the rituals.

Love had no rituals. It was easy to give, easy to receive and hard to get.

Forget religion. Love selflessly.

******

CHAPTER 7
LESS IS MORE

It was the life of the have-nots that always fascinated me.

It was six pm when I went to call our maid from her home. She lived in a small thatched hut in a slum near a dirty pond.

It was dark when I reached her home, walking over the loose granite stones that bordered the pond.

I opened the door to their one-room hut.

Her kids, Mohini and Girija, were eating their dinner under a kerosene lamp.

It was kind-of like a non-romantic candlelit dinner. The bleak light filled the sole room of their home.

They had very little to call belongings. Just few clothes were crumpled on one side.

A few objects. No tables, chairs or furniture of any kind.

There were a few white metal plates with dark-blue rims – this was quite fashionable among the poorer folks then. Every beggar had them. I do not know why or where they bought them from.

They were eating rice from a metal plate. Next to it there was just one smaller metal plate with a bit of chili-powder mixed with a bit of oil and a bit of salt.

The red chili-paste was the only thing they had to hide the blandness of rice.

Under the lamplight, the scene slowly etched itself into my forever memory.

I yearned for the chili sauce they had.

It was something I had never had.

I wanted something they would gladly do without.

I sat down with them on the cold floor. "Can I taste a bit?" I asked them.

"Absolutely, here you go," the sisters said, moving the plates slightly closer to me, with innocent smiles on their face.

They shared with me. I took a small bit of the rice, dipped it in the chili paste, and ate it.

It was one of the happiest meals I had ever had and better than any banquet I have ever had since, because it was all they had, and they had shared it with me without any hesitation.

It was a candlelit dinner, no caviar and no salmon.

A bit of chili powder, a bit of salt, and a bit of oil. That was all.

Sometimes I still make that chili sauce for myself when I am alone. The recipe is easy, quick and cheap.

I've found that adding a bit of vinegar or a few thin slices of red shallots makes it taste more interesting. Replacing the rice with simple boiled Yucca Root is also recommended.

The most blessed ones are the simplest of all.

******

CHAPTER 8
LIFE AS WE KNOW IT

My Aunt Ann died. Her child was now an orphan.

Everyone had wanted her to pass away peacefully, as she suffered from a chronic disease. But when she died, everyone cried.

I wondered how the bodies could be reassembled if we had to resurrect them.

What exactly happened when they were buried in the grave? Would they suffocate? Would Dracula come by to suck their blood?

Why did people want Aunt Ann to die if they would be sad to see her dead?

Live well when you are alive. Stop worrying about the life after.

******

I wandered around among the graves in the cemetery, reading the epitaphs of all those who had left over the years.

Some had died young. Many had died old.

Some shared graves. Husbands and wives – mixed in the same earth.

My cousin showed me the "bone pit" where they dropped the leftover bones whenever they cleared a grave.

It was an endless, dark pit. Once family and friends stopped visiting, they needed to make room for the new dead people.

Everything transforms.

******

I saw folks giving their last kisses to my dead aunt through a white handkerchief that was laid over her face.

My dad asked me to give my last kiss.

I was never close to the aunt. "Why should I?" I asked.

"You will never see her again," he said.

"Okay," I said, and I kneeled and kissed her for the first and last time.

It was like kissing a stone – a cold stone.

Normally we care only about people who are close to us. There are other humans deserving of love.

******

CHAPTER 9
THE DARKEST DAY

The newspapers had been filled with the news of the upcoming solar eclipse. Never look directly at the sun. Cover your windows. If you want to look at the sun, use a thick dark solar filter.

So on it went.

My dad was very tense; almost like a nuclear war was coming.

I could not buy a solar filter. It was way too expensive.

Someone told me that a safe way to watch the eclipse was to fill a tub of water, darken it by mixing the water with cow dung, and to look at the reflection.

So I went to collect cow dung. It was a horrible task, but I wanted to see the eclipse.

The hour was approaching. My dad had covered the whole house with blankets. Every window was covered. It was dark inside.

I snuck out the collection of cow dung mixed with water and pushed the tub out.

I peeped through the sheets covering the window at the reflection of the sun in the darkened water.

The sun was being eaten up by a dark circle.

An eerie silence. The world stood still.

Then the brighter sun started to reemerge.

My dad did not like me looking at the reflection in a cow dung pool. He asked me to go and wash my hands with soap and water.

But I needed to see my first solar eclipse.

I remembered the stories of natives who had been fooled by conquerors about an upcoming solar eclipse.

I wondered if the natives had been totally unaware of eclipses, since some of them must have seen eclipses at least once in a while.

Lack of tools should not stop a curious mind.

******

CHAPTER 10
SUPERMAN

I collected tips from my grocery trips to buy tickets to go and see a new movie –"Superman".

Flying through the clouds, Christopher Reeves was awesome. I loved the curl of hair that dropped over his forehead, like a new moon.

When I left the theater, I looked into the mirror on my dad's bicycle. I made a curl of hair on my forehead.

I felt like Superman, like I could fly.

I started riding the bike.

Faster and faster. I was moving so fast that the rest of the world looked like a blur. I was Superman, without the cape, but I had the curl.

I turned curves, banking the bike heavily.

I extended my hands forward, just like Superman.

I could actually ride the bike without my hands on the handlebars.

My space flight came to an abrupt halt when a rickshaw in front of me suddenly turned to pick up a passenger.

The fall was so bad that I did not want to be a superman again. I needed yet another career path.

Real life hurts.

******

I loved movies.

Bud Spencer and Terrence Hill were fun. Like Laurel and Hardy. One fat. One thin.

Bud could whip anybody. Terrence was cool.

They were an awesome pair.

Herbie and Benjie. Bruce Lee and Richard Saxon.

Bruce Lee could kick people out of the water. For months I chopped my hand at walls. I wished someday I could buy a *nanchaku* like Bruce and fight off the bad guys. Someday I would be able to afford the hundreds of rupees to teach myself karate. I would get my black belt.

I watched Chinese movies with fighters acting like tigers, snakes and mongooses. They poked out each other's eyes and chopped each other up with large knives and swords. The actors twisted and turned and stood bending backwards – like a tableau that changed every few seconds.

"The Sound of Music" showed a perfect family in a beautiful but imperfect world. The mountains and the music were awe-inspiring.

I wished I were one of the Von Trapp family and that I lived with those blue mountains and the streams and the sounds of music.

But there was the evil of Hitler and the Nazis. Hitler's Nazi emblem looked like the Indian Swastika.

The Von Trapp Story was not unlike what had happened in 1947 with India and Pakistan. Not until Ayodhya in the 1990s did I think something like that could happen in a country like India anymore.

Animals can never be human. Humans can be animals.

******

CHAPTER 11
BAD OMEN

Teens are impressionable.

"The Omen" was a movie I had wanted to watch for weeks and finally I was able to collect enough money to go to see it.

Unfortunately, I picked a second show that ended at midnight.

The trip home in the dark was eerie.

I heard several dogs barking, fighting and running towards where I was. I froze on my bicycle.

Luckily, they passed me. But I was scared beyond imagination.

I watched carefully while I went around trucks. I just wanted to make sure none of them got loose and moved towards me to decapitate me – like what had happened to the photographer in the movie.

Every alley looked dark and foreboding.

I woke up no one when I reached home. And I went to bed.

It was two am. I woke up. I heard Damien calling me, saw him standing next to me.

I almost fainted.

I screamed. Got up, and screamed again. And then put the lights on.

It was my brother.

Your dreams can come true. Your nightmares can come true.

******

"The Exorcist" was scarier than "The Omen." The girl in the movie vomited bluish stuff and turned her head in a semicircle. It was way too much for me.

My sister closely resembled Regan MacNeil – the demonic, possessed child in the movie – though my sister had normal eyes and darker skin.

47

She would scream, turn her head like in the movie and give me that cold stare.

She sometimes snuck up on me when I was trying to do my homework at night, and acted like Regan.

She knew how to scare me well.

I wished I had a better brother and sister than Damien and Regan.

I started wearing a cross on a black string all the time on my neck to ward away my two weird siblings.

Only you are a normal child – if you are a member of a normal family.

******

CHAPTER 12
HUMAN SACRIFICE

"*Yakshi* will come to you at midnight. Dressed in a white *sari*. Beautiful she will be," Grandma said. She loved the local legend of the *Yakshi*, the female vampires who tempted people and sucked their blood and killed them.

And I loved the stories that Grandma told. I moved closer to her, feeling a bit scared.

"*Yakshi* lives under the *Pala Tree*. She will come to the victim and ask for *chunnambu* (a white lime paste). Suddenly she will transform herself into a ghost, and come closer and suck your blood."

"To kill a *Yakshi*, you have to drive a nail through its heart. A cross sometimes does the trick," Grandma continued, as I slept off.

Some humans are worse than Yakshis.

******

Ezhilam Pala (Alstonia scholaris) is a tree with white flowers that emit a haunting smell. Its leaves form a beautiful seven-leaf pattern. Its bark gives out a milky white substance if cut, much like the *chunnambu* that *Yakshis* ask for.

I knew one Pala tree in the neighborhood.

I picked up some Pala flowers once, on my way home. I put four of them in my left pocket. When I reached home, they had disappeared. This was so spooky that I never went under a Pala tree again.

I heard Raghu had a mental breakdown and almost died after he met a *Yakshi* at the local park. I knew he was a strong kid. But I had never seen a *Yakshi*. I never really wanted to see one, either.

Fear fear.

******

"*Chunnambu undo* (Do you have some *chunnambu*)?" asked my little sister in a low voice. She was looking at my neck with her big beautiful eyes and she wore a white frock.

I was doing my homework that evening. I did not want to reply so I got up and switched on brighter lights.

It was getting dark.

"Hi hi hi…" she giggled, and walked off. She knew exactly how to scare her elder brother.

******

I remembered Grandma's words. "A *Yakshi* will become human if you drive a nail through her heart."

I hatched a plan to permanently get rid of the problem. After all, it is not unusual to expect others to be normal.

I went to the storeroom at the back of our home. I opened the hardware box and found a small rusty nail. There were two hammers. I chose the little one, for the little nail. It was an iron hammer with a wooden handle. It smelled of rust.

I took the hammer and the nail to the front room. I held them in my hands.

It was six pm. The evening was kind of warm. It was getting darker. The day was ending and the night was starting.

******

I kneeled in front of a picture of Jesus. My mom had lit a perfumed candle, and the pleasing smell wafted through the air. I moved a table to the front of the photo, below where we used to keep the Bible.

I called my sister. She came in. She did not notice the nail or the hammer.

I said I had devised a new game. "Do you want to play?" I asked.

She was always ready for playing games. She preferred games to reading books.

"Lie down on this table," I said, "and close your eyes."

She obeyed me. That was very unusual for her.

"Act like you are sleeping for the next few minutes," I said. I took the nail in my left hand and the hammer in my right hand. I was right handed.

"Do you want *chunnambu*?" I asked my sister, to check if she still wanted to be a *Yakshi*.

"Yes," she hissed, without opening her eyes.

I took the nail close to her chest. And I held the hammer above it.

I looked at Jesus' eyes. He looked kind, and forgiving.

My sister still kept her eyes closed. I started to hit the nail on its head.

I heard my mom calling for me and I was suddenly distracted.

Still, the hammer hit the nail, though not as hard as I wanted to.

"*Ente Ammo* (my mother)," my sister screamed. Her eyes opened wide and she looked terrified. She was certainly in a lot of pain. There was blood on her chest.

The nail was too blunt.

My mother came running. She looked at the scene and fainted.

We spent the rest of the night at the hospital. Shots for tetanus, and such.

My sister never scared me again and still has the scar to prove it.

And from then on she refused to play any game in which she had to close her eyes.

Try not to scare anyone. Kids, please never try these things at home!

******

Both Damien and Regan grew up to be normal human beings. Much later in life.

Without any more sacrifices.

People change. For better or for worse.

******

CHAPTER 13
EVIL INCARNATE

Every kid grows up among adults.

Not all adults have good intentions.

Park Anthony seemed to be a friend of all my friends.

He was unusually dark, fat and always around kids.

He promised them candy, books, even birds – parrots and love birds. He asked us to come to his home, or to the top floor of the public library, where it was quiet.

And he said it was fun.

Some of my friends talked to him for hours. It was almost beyond my understanding.

Park Anthony promised to give me a dove and a puppy, if only my sister and I would come and visit him. I was too small; I was a kid who innocently and obediently believed anyone who was older than me.

He asked me again to come with my sister to his home. I felt there was something unusual about him; I didn't know why. Luckily, I never went. I just stayed away.

From others I heard that this guy was not a friend; he was someone you could not trust. Whatever that meant...

I saw Park Anthony several years later when I was much older and much wiser.

He came towards me as soon as he saw me. "Hello," he said and crept closer towards me with a grin.

"Stay away," I warned him. His grin vanished.

There is no need to trust anyone. Trust yourself and your instincts. Just say no if you are uncomfortable about anyone or anything, even if they may make you feel obliged to listen to them.

******

CHAPTER 14
ETERNAL
ENTREPRENEUR

Entrepreneurship was natural to my mother.

At a time when women's rights were starting to be more recognized, she teamed with her friends to form a home-based food company that made jams, preserves and jellies.

They named their company *Matha Foods* in reverence to Mother Mary. Their business plan was written on the back of a piece of paper. There was such demand for good jam. They could possibly sell thousands of bottles of jams to the local vendors and make thousands of rupees.

They purchased the equipment and materials and organized everything. They pumped the gas stove and started the fire. Gallons of hot oil formed waves on the large tub-like pan; ready to fry whatever they wanted to fry.

And my brother came along, the Damien incarnate, playing catch-me-if-you-can with two of his neighbors.

He was running fast.

He stepped over a tall step, jumped over the women who were attending to the large pan of frying oil and landed right into the frying pan.

The pan, the women and the Damien incarnate fell into the fire and then there was hot oil, fire, and screaming women everywhere.

Little Damien had severe burns.

The enterprise that the women had dreamed of had gone up in smoke.

A business plan never accounts for acts of the Anti-Christ.

******

Entrepreneurship among the women did not die. They wanted to help their husbands get rich fast.

Cocoa was being touted as the great crop at the time; there was a great market for cocoa seeds, from which chocolates are made. But there was a scarcity of the seeds and the prices shot up. One pod of seeds could fetch you Rs. 4. And a small cocoa plant cost Rs. 5.

If you could grow the plant, it could yield dozens of cocoa pods. If you planted some more of the cocoa plants, you could make a big business of cocoa plantations, for which you needed land.

But if they at least had a few cocoa plants the women could use them as a springboard to the endgame, which was to have a cocoa plantation.

I was recruited to go and buy four cocoa plants. I took my dad's beautiful bicycle to the horticulturist and purchased the plants. I tied them around the bike. The dynamo-powered bicycle lamp led me home with its feeble light. It was 7 pm when I reached home.

It was an awesome feeling to plant the small cocoa plants in our backyard. I imagined them growing tall in months, full of cocoa pods – almost like money trees.

I dreamed of cocoa plantations. We had to start looking for some land to cultivate more of the cocoa plants.

In the morning I woke up to my mother's screams.

Everyone came out running to see what had happened.

All four cocoa plants had been cut down overnight, right above the root by rats.

Unexpected events and disasters are guaranteed to happen in any business. Factor failures into the possible results, along with the castles in the air.

******

CHAPTER 15
ROCKET SCIENCE

Physics fascinated me. Gravity. Rockets.

Kerala State gets its name from coconuts.

I loved the baby coconuts that fell off our rich neighbor's coconut tree into our yard. I gathered them every morning.

And played with them. Peeled off their shells. Dug inside the brown and white matter.

I collected the brown matter and made it into a paste. I would apply the paste to my forehead – like the sandal paste (*chandanam*) some Hindus wore. I went around chanting, "Ram, Ram…"

And I would pull out the pinnae (*ola*, a single leaf with a vein through the middle) from the coconut fronds (*ola madal*), the long nicely patterned leaves of the coconut tree. I then pulled out the vein (*eerkil*) of those pinnae. Some made brooms out of these veins by tying them together, and though thin they were rather strong, especially when dried.

I had the idea of sticking a pinnae vein into the soft brown head of a baby coconut. I made it like a rocket.

It looked more like Sputnik, albeit with just one long tail. I wanted to see how high I could send it. Like a ball and chain, I held the pinnae vein on one hand, started moving my hand in circles.

As the baby coconut picked up speed, it slowly turned into a circular blur. It had enough speed to go quite high, I thought. And I released the baby coconut rocket.

And the baby coconut rocket with a pinnae vein tail rose against gravity.

The release was firm and perfect; I was proud of its flight path. I dreamed that someday I would join the

ISRO (Indian Space Research Organization) and make rockets and missiles.

Mrs. Leela, my neighbor, was cleaning her backyard with a broom made of pinnae veins – cut midway to have a sharp, horizontal edge at the bottom. These natural brooms leave a pattern on the ground that looks like a snow angel made by a one-winged angel.

The baby coconut rocket rose against all expectations – higher and higher it went. It rose past the trees in an arc.

For a moment, it looked as if it paused at the top of its flight path. And then, it started its descent.

Slowly the rocket turned – head first, then tail, picking up speed.

It had gone way above the canopy of the surrounding mango trees and now it reentered the mango leaf zone. It made a slight noise as it sped past the raw green mangoes and bright yellow leaves.

The baby coconut rocket kept on gathering speed.

It was not headed for our backyard – it had crossed beyond our walls.

"*Ente Amme* (my holy mother)!" A scream penetrated the morning. The baby coconut rocket had landed on Mrs. Leela's head, knocking her almost unconscious.

Mrs. Lilly, Mrs. Valsamma, and my mother all came running out of their respective homes to see what had happened. Mrs. Leela was on the ground.

The baby coconut had separated from the tail, I noticed. No one could track the weapon that had almost killed Mrs. Leela.

I acted like I knew nothing. It was my neighbor's baby coconut. It was my neighbor's pinnae vein. And it was in my neighbor's yard. Who would have wanted to hurt Mrs. Leela?

Mrs. Leela had lost consciousness.

The weapon was never traced back to me.

Some took it as an act of God, a punishment for Mrs. Leela's gossips.

She recovered well, but slowly.

What goes up must come down. Plan the whole flight path. But, whatever your plans are, things can and will go wrong. You simply have no choice on the laws of physics, especially gravity.

******

CHAPTER 16
LITTLE LIFE

I loved rabbits. They were small, cute, unemotional and furry – with their eager red eyes. They ate banana tree leaves. And their cages smelled funny. They didn't stink, but had a vegetarian smell.

My dad had hired a carpenter to build a rabbit cage. When we got our new rabbit that afternoon, we installed the rabbit cage near a window ledge – safe from all kinds of predators.

I fed the rabbit banana leaves. It nibbled it out of my hand. I spent the whole evening with my new friend.

I made plans for my rabbit and I for the next day.

I had recently bought a book about rabbits living on a carrot farm. I wanted to feed my rabbit carrots, but we didn't have any. I thought I could get some the next day from the market – I wanted to make sure the carrots came with some leaves so that the rabbit would find it easy to eat – just like in my rabbit book.

The next morning I woke up early.

The bright sun was shining on our front porch.

The welcome mat in our front room had some entrails spread over it.

Strange, it looked.

The rabbit cage had been pushed down from the backyard windowsill. Its door was open and the rabbit was gone.

You can only lose what you love or possess.

******

My dad noticed a dog trying to escape through a hole nearby.

The dog had pushed the cage down, and devoured the rabbit.

I think it did not like the taste of intestines.

My dad called our neighbors.

The dog was in the hole between our two homes. The neighbors got a long crowbar, and impaled it right through.

The dog had white fur and black spots.

No one wanted to see the dog alive.

Kill and be killed. It looked like that was the law of nature.

One needed food. The other needed its life.

Life is fair. Life is not fair.

******

CHAPTER 17
LESSONS FROM THE
FISH MARKET

Cochin market is next to the church and is a place of constant action, intense business and folks who focus on selling. Women sell fish caught in the nearby lake. Men sell vegetables from Tamil Nadu. Customers love to bargain, even with fair prices.

I somehow never bargained. I would not buy if the price didn't seem right.

I would get 10 paisa if I went to the market to get the daily items. I used the money to buy *chandrakkaran* (mangoes) – the cute sweet ones.

Fish were cheap, but you had to be careful while buying. Lift the gill of the fish and see if it is blood red. If it is black the fish may be bad. One day I was in a hurry and I forgot to check – I think I trusted the seller.

Halfway home, I realized something fishy was going on. The fish smelled bad. I checked, and there it was. Gills as black as tar. I had been taken for a ride.

Back at the market, the guy wouldn't even look at me. He kept selling. I was angry, so I took the fish and dumped it into his basket.

"Why did you do that?" he asked me.

"The fish you sold me are horrible," I said.

"I only sell good fish," he retorted.

"Yeah, right," I said.

"And you dumped all that fish into my basket of good fish? I do not even know you," he screamed.

I was a kid. He could not kill me.

I noticed that the person who actually sold me the fish was standing in a nearby stall, laughing at me. He kept on selling his bad fish.

Caveat Emptor (let the buyer beware), they say.

It is a mistake to act too fast.

******

I was showing our new servant, Raghu, how to go to *Neena Cold Storage* to buy cocktail sausages and fish *kheema*. I walked with him all the way to make sure he knew every turn and street to get there. It usually takes about a half-hour to get there from our home.

The next day it took Raghu about four hours to come back from the store. He had gotten lost and could not find the store.

"What happened?" I asked. "I showed you street by street how to get there."

"I could not find the red car in front of the store today," he responded, innocently.

Never underestimate stupidity. Or innocence.

******

CHAPTER 18
WORLD GOING
BACKWARDS

Our school was in the midst of hills. Mostly, we would take the school bus back and forth.

Our school had three busses: *Patta*, the oldest; *Tata*, the next; and *Moota*, the last.

Moota was a refurbished bus from the Department of State Transport – it looked like it had previously belonged to some jail to carry around criminals.

Tata was the youngest of the three buses and *Paili*, who was a daredevil driver, drove it. It was special to travel in the *Tata* school bus because it was sleek, cool and fast. Folks who came by that regularly had an air about themselves.

I loved watching the rest of the world from the school bus.

As we sped up, the rocks and grass moved back faster and faster into blurry streaks.

It was fun sitting next to the noisy engine of the bus, feeling the warmth of its hot air, especially when it was raining, to compensate the cold air on our faces.

Everyone had special marked seats in the bus. Window seats were in demand. Having a window seat meant a better view during the trip and control of the window shutters in the rain.

I heard one of the students who sat in a seat nearby had a bout with Tuberculosis, and though he had been cured, I held my breath when he was nearby. I did not want to get Tuberculosis and die; that was how Aunt Ann had died.

******

After the school is over for the day I sometimes walked to the nearby bus stop to take a private bus. Bus stops were usually filled with students, whom the buses avoid picking up, since they paid a very little fare compared to fatter adults, who paid in full.

The bus stop was at the foot of a hill and there were lots of schools nearby. Lots of girls from the nearby school would be at the same place waiting for a bus. Once I saw a friend of mine, Sajan, coming down the hill on his rented bike. In those days, you could rent bicycles for about 10 paisa per hour.

Something seemed wrong.

He was coming faster than I would have expected, trying to show off to the girls how well and fast he could ride the bike.

He certainly had everyone's attention. He came down fast, banking the bicycle a bit, getting ready to take the turn.

And he turned.

Or, it looked like he attempted to turn. He turned the handle. But the bike did not turn with him. The screws were loose.

Sajan and the bike landed right on the bunch of girls who may otherwise have been impressed by his demonstration.

Do not try stunts with rented bicycles. Check your equipment before attempting a stunt.

******

CHAPTER 19
LIFE EXPERIMENTS

Thomas Alva Edison always fascinated me. A great and prolific inventor, he started life as a newspaper boy. Later, he made his own laboratory, where he conducted experiments.

I was inspired to start my own laboratory. I was around the age Edison was when he was a newspaper boy. So I too wanted to be a scientist.

I decided to buy some chemicals to do experiments. Salt and baking soda were not impressive enough. I finally settled on iodine. I went to a lab supply store and they quoted Rs. 70 per bottle of Iodine. That was way beyond my budget.

My approach was simple. What would happen if I tried something? There was no particular objective – just do an experiment and see what happened.

So I turned to electricity. I finally found a string of Christmas lights in the storeroom that had been damaged.

It was 8 pm and the whole neighborhood was having their dinner.

I took one bulb out of the string, with the two wires sticking out in both directions. I found an electrical outlet, with deadly 220V electricity.

It had just two holes for plugs to plug in.

The small bulb I had had two wires sticking out of it.

The scientist in me cooked up an experiment.

What will happen if we put these two wires into the electric sockets?

Would the bulb shine brighter?

And by how much?

As soon as I inserted the wires into the sockets, there was a flash from the holes, and the whole neighborhood went black. The fuse to the entire neighborhood had gone bust.

I decided experiments were too dangerous a game to play. I needed another career path.

Do not play with fire. Do not play with wires.

******

Riyaz, our neighbor, was an expert with electronic devices. He made radios and other devices by himself with components he bought from the store.

Riyaz wanted to play a trick on his cousin, Ahmed.

Ahmed was sitting on a bed and Riyaz asked him to touch a live wire, if he dared.

Ahmed did, and nothing happened to him – because he was not touching the ground.

Ahmed just smiled at Riyaz, and said that the wire must not be live.

Then Riyaz whispered in my ear. If you touch Ahmed, he will get a shock. So I did.

The circuit was now closed. The wire was live. Ahmed. Me. The ground.

Electricity at 220 Volts feels somewhat weird. It can actually kill you. The fuse box went off, instantly saving the two of us.

Never try to help someone else who is trying to kill another person.

******

CHAPTER 20
OHM'S LAW

"Ohm's law is nothing but I=V/R," rumbled Mr. Thomas, our physics teacher. He somehow managed to structure every sentence around the phrase "nothing but".

V/R=I. We. Are. I.

I parsed the equation in a peculiar way to commit it to my forever memory.

Ohm = Om.

Om. Aum. The mystical syllable in most Eastern religions, chanted by the holy men. Like *Amen* and *Amin* in Middle-Eastern religions.

A few of us started whispering. Om… Om...

At first it was a whisper. Then it became almost harmonic. I started saying it faster.

Om… Om… Ohm… Ohm…

"Ohm… Ohm… Ohm's Law… Ohm's Law..." we chanted. Slowly at first. The whisper turned into a chant, slower again, then louder and faster.

More friends heard the divine syllable being invoked and some others joined the chant. "Ohm... Ohm... Ohm's Law... Ohm's Law..."

The whole section started chanting, with their hands covering their mouths. No one could see exactly who was chanting and who was not.

In a short time, the whole class was chanting, "Ohm's Law... Ohm's Law..."

In a few more minutes, a few more classes next to us started the chant.

In a few more minutes, the whole section of our school had joined the chant.

In a few more minutes, the whole school was chanting.

Invoking the Law of the Divine Syllable.

I had figured out how to start a movement – how to make the masses move.

I could get into politics someday, I thought.

Like Indira Gandhi.

The secret was simple. Keep it short. Make it sound good. Give the masses something to chant.

You do not need any substance to move masses. You can control the world with just a chant that sounds good.

******

CHAPTER 21
LEADERSHIP

In many parts of the world, leadership is confused with a stern commanding voice and goon-like behavior toward following minions.

I was the only cadet in the student Cadet Corps that wore a cap with a black pom-pom. Everyone else had red pom-poms.

I was tall, so the instructor assumed that I would be able to command.

He called three of us – Rajiv, Suresh and I – to try out to be squadron leaders. There were just two spots.

Rajiv had an almost synthetic commanding voice. The squadron did exactly as he said.

Suresh commanded and the squadron did exactly as told.

This was going to be easy, I thought.

"Straight, set, march," I commanded the squadron. They did exactly as I asked.

They kept on marching.

"Ask them to turn right," the instructor said.

"Turn right," I commanded. And the squadron turned right, and kept marching.

"Left, right, left, right…" went the squadron.

"Get them to turn back," the instructor said.

The winds had shifted during this time. I was facing the wind. And the squadron was marching away from me.

"About turn," I commanded.

The squadron went on marching without listening to me.

"About turn," I commanded again.

The squadron continued marching and took no notice of me.

"Get them to turn back," the instructor repeated.

"I said, about turn," in the loudest voice I could.

The squadron continued marching, deaf as you could imagine.

The winds carried my voice north and the squadron was headed south.

My soldiers were heading towards the edge of the playground. If not stopped, they would fall off the edge.

I started running after the squadron. I ran ahead of the group and raised my hand and asked them to stop.

"About turn," I commanded, as best I could.

The squadron did turn this time.

But my instructor had already chosen the two squadron leaders.

I was not one of them.

I was tall enough, but I did not have the voice of a leader.

From then on I believed that I would never be able to command anything. I had lost confidence.

If you have a melodious voice, join a choir – not the army.

******

CHAPTER 22
HOW NOT TO
SHOW UP

Every teenager wants attention.

Abraham, who was my most fashionable classmate, wanted to be a cowboy.

He wore blue jeans, blue shirt, a Texas hat – and leather shoes to boot.

In a mid-sized city like Cochin, this was a rarity.

He wore a belt complete with a gun holster, without the gun, which would have made it illegal.

He kind of had the looks of Yul Brenner in "The Magnificent Seven." Square jaws, thin lips, faint eyebrows and thin hair.

If you asked his name, he would just say "Ay-br-um" – with a nod.

He was a decent teen, just full of style. Like a hero from Louis L'Amor westerns, even though he lacked a real horse.

Blue jeans were a fashion only a few of the rich kids could afford.

There were those, like Santhosh, who walked with legs curved and with steps crooked, imagining they were cowboys looking for some damsel in distress, instead of looking after real cows like they were supposed to.

Blue jeans somehow said it all.

It was the in thing.

Hippie styles and Bruce Lee step cuts were outdated.

Jeans were in, and short hair.

People measured how hip you were by asking the width of your pants bottom. It was not cool to have bells more than 25 inches in width. Gone were the days of 36 to 45 inches; bells that looked almost like skirts.

All rich kids had to wear blue jeans. I needed one, so I asked my mom. She was worried, as if wearing jeans meant that I would somehow turn immoral.

"Well," I said, "I topped the recent exams. I'm doing fine in school."

"Okay, but you should not get involved with bad friends," she warned.

"I've saved coins for about Rs. 200. Can I can use that?"

"Okay," she agreed.

Finally, I went to the *Sunayna Jean Shop* with a bunch of coins in my pocket. The salesman was good. He sold me blue jeans, a jacket, and a leather belt for Rs. 150. "You look very cool in that," he said, closing the deal.

Eager buyer is an easier sell.

******

81

The next day, everyone in the school looked surprised. I had finally become cool, and they accepted it. Some girls laughed at me, but I thought they were just envious.

I could not focus on what teachers were trying to teach in class. Mr. Thomas, our chemistry professor, said to me, "You look very restless today."

"*Ja*," I said, in German.

"Did you turn in your lab report today?" he asked.

"*Nyet*," I answered, in Russian.

I wanted to be everything except a lad from Cochin.

As the day wore on, I actually did grow restless. I did not have the holster like Abraham did, though.

At the end of the day, after I was sure that the entire school had noticed me in my blue jeans and jacket, it was time to go home.

Pearson, the most fashionable and the next coolest guy in school after Abraham, came up to me as I was leaving and whispered in my ear.

"A friendly piece of advice. The blue jeans you are wearing are very cool. You may want to make sure that you fold your zipper the other way when you zip your fly. It is open."

Always remember to make sure that the zipper has folded back after you have closed it so it does not slip down.

I never wanted to act cool again. Never again, in my life.

Just be normal.

******

CHAPTER 23
ART OF THE APE

When you look for a job, extra-curricular achievements are a measure of how interesting you are as a candidate. I needed certificates to prove I was good at something.

I hoped I could someday get a certificate so that I would be able to walk across the stage on the school anniversary – which I knew would make my father proud.

I could sing, so I joined the song competition at school.

"Life is a bubble," I sang. It was a beautiful song, with beautiful words. The audience was silent. I saw everyone looking solely at me.

And I forgot the next line.

In fact, I forgot the rest of the song.

Then I laughed, right into the microphone. The amplified laugh spread throughout the auditorium.

The audience laughed. I laughed again.

I looked around for my song sheet and I completed my song.

Later some said that I did sing very well. Mine was the best.

But I got no prize, and no certificate.

My dad could not be proud of me that year, again.

Remember the cheat-sheet.

******

My friend, Prasad, is a professional mimicry artist. I finally got him to teach me how to perform.

He taught me how to make the sound of a galloping horse.

Sound of a ringing gunshot.

Screams of a woman in distress.

Of a waterfall.

Of a hurricane.

Of a rock music concert.

I became quite good at making all kinds of noises.

Finally, the day of the competition came.

I performed a pop music concert. The drums, guitar, and the song, all performed by me, simultaneously.

It was good. The audience was silent. Then I heard the thunderous applause.

My first mimicry performance was successful.

I got to Part II. I mimicked a Western Movie Trailer.

I made it sound like a desert, with a horse galloping from the horizon. The horse whinnied. A gun shot. The sound echoed around the auditorium. Sounds of more gunshots followed. I made background music to spice things up.

Then I came to the part of the trailer that listed the actors.

I drew a blank; I had completely forgotten the names. I thought I would list the Magnificent Seven Actors but I could not remember any of them at that moment.

I said, "Starring Ranjit George Thampi", while looking at Ranjit.

I started picking the names of folks from the audience.

"*Ay-br-um* Varghese."

Horse whinnied. Gunshot again.

"Directed by Pearson," I closed the credits.

"Coming to theaters this November," I concluded.

Gun shots again. The sound of a tornado – or a hurricane – or howling wind.

The performance was a complete success.

I came in second, just short of being nominated to the state level.

But most importantly, I learned one thing.

Before any stage performance, even the smallest details should be rehearsed. Do not innovate during a performance or demo, unless something goes terribly wrong.

******

CHAPTER 24
DREAMER AND HIS DREAM

I already had a dream girl. In fact, I never thought she would be mine, even in a dream. So I started looking at other choices.

Seeta was a normal girl. She looked like she was straight out of a cartoon.

She was very fair, with dark hair and was thin like a pen and kind of tall. An egg-shaped face. She always wore black dresses and jasmine flowers. An average girl, and all her friends were considered much prettier.

She never looked at me.

Maybe she was blind.

I was intent on being the best in academics. I had been topping my class. But Seeta bothered me.

Once in a while, my mind wandered over to her. I wasn't sure if this was normal.

Mr. Varadarajan was my physics teacher – an exceptional one.

I asked him, "Is it normal to think about a girl when trying to learn physics or chemistry?"

"No," he said, "let us focus on physics."

But he looked at me as if I were a strange kid.

Well, that was the end of Seeta. I started not noticing her anymore.

Other people are just humans.

******

Everyone wants to be noticed. But no one seemed to notice me: a shy nerd, a quiet geek, a lanky kid, always with a book in his hand.

It was the last day of college.

We elected the most popular girl. A Muslim girl named Abba won. Many of the prettier girls lost.

The most popular boy election was next. I voted for Anand. He was good at singing and he was rich. He was also my best friend – since the first grade.

The votes came in.

"You are the most popular boy," the verdict declared.

"All the girls voted for you," someone told me.

I was surprised.

Nerds get the best. Be happy when someone calls you a geek. Everyone will notice you.

******

CHAPTER 25
WEDDING BELLS

My cousin was getting married to the love of her life.

Her brother, James, was in charge of the *thali*, a little locket that signified holy matrimony. The bridegroom takes the *thali* on a thin thread around the bride's neck, ties a knot and they are man and wife.

The marriage ceremony was in full swing.

"Do you take this person to be your wife in holy matrimony?" the priest asked.

"I absolutely do," said the bridegroom.

And the bride returned the favor, in a low demure voice.

"Please tie the *thali* on the bride," said Fr. Antony.

The bridegroom looked at James.

James looked back.

James had completely forgotten about the *thali*. He had left it at home. His ride to the wedding was late and he did not have the time to remember.

The marriage could not proceed.

Women always wear their *thali* to indicate their commitment to their marriage.

My mom took her *thali* and offered to step in.

The marriage took place with my mom's *thali*.

Some people are not dependable. Factor that into planning.

******

The marriage feast was almost ready.

Thousands were at the marriage and they were to be treated to the best *Biriyani*, a spicy rice dish mixed with finely cooked meat.

"Why does this vinegar smell like kerosene?" asked a helper, smelling the waft from the bottle. He needed to add vinegar into the *Biriyani* to round out the wonderful smelling spices.

He emptied the vinegar into the almost-cooked *Biriyani*.

But the bottle was actually full of kerosene. Someone had mislabeled the bottle. The *Biriyani* was no longer edible.

The feast was a disaster. Everyone had to start from the beginning and the whole thing was delayed by another three hours.

Stupid things can happen at the very last moment. Watch out for those.

******

CHAPTER 26
Y?

The first time I saw a Rubik's cube, I thought it was impossible to solve. In another month, I was solving it under a minute.

Mr. Komalan, a math teacher, told me that I should try to get into the Indian Institute of Technology, the IIT.

IITs were technical schools considered to have the highest admission standards in the world.

But I just wanted to attend an engineering school for normal folks.

Do not limit yourself. Aim high. You will most likely get where you aim at.

******

A physics teacher, who had such passion for teaching, once told me – "Always ask Y. Why is the hibiscus flower red? Why is the sky blue?"

That one piece of advice changed my life fundamentally.

I thought about everything.

About the trees.

The earth.

The stars.

The sun.

The moon.

The galaxies.

The universe.

The worm.

The rain.

The clouds.

Water.

Air. Fire. Sulfur.

Carbon.

And, yes, the hibiscus flower.

"Just ask why," he said.

Question folks about everything.

Acquire undying curiosity. Try to explain everything.

Seek answers – selflessly and constantly. Be arrogant about seeking the unknown.

Be humble about recognizing the forces that run this universe.

That is, if this is the only universe.

Suddenly, everything became questionable.

Questions triggered more questions.

Gone out the window was the concept of settled life – based on religion and myth.

Question everything.

******

Church turned confusing to me.

Rituals made no sense.

Even lack of rituals made no sense.

The mosques I went to were too empty to be impressive.

95

Temples I went to were too full of stone gods for me to feel comfortable.

I knew somewhere at the back of my mind that the divine existed – just not in a way that I could see it and not in the way others claimed to see it.

Understand more about rituals.

******

Still I went to church services. Just to see my dream girl, hoping that she would also be at the same service by chance.

Sermons were packed in beautiful language, expounding morality and telling us how to formulate thought – somehow constraining thoughts that might offend faith.

The lack of real substance disappointed me.

The stress seemed to be on belief – not discovery.

Searching, with church-approved blinders on.

Seek and you shall find.

******

CHAPTER 27
Y NOT?

It was my first week at IIT, Madras.

It was Raj who asked me the innocent question, "Y not?"

"What do you mean, Y not?" I asked.

"Because Y not is the initial value of Y," he quipped.

Ask why. Ask why not.

******

IITians are known for their fun side. Some like Raj, were constantly funny.

Raj was great at photography. He ran the Film Society, where he selected and screened films at the OAT (Open Air Theater) – a Saturday night ritual for all at IIT, Madras.

IIT hostels have some very funny people, and some strange and scary ones.

Aero was a serious guy and wanted to be the best soccer goalie in the world. He asked anyone who would listen to kick a soccer ball at an imaginary goal post, so he could attempt to save it. Aero was not too good at this.

Few folks like being a goalie. I found Aero very curious. He was certainly strange.

Once, another crazy IITian locked him up in a room. In an hour, Aero had gotten out of the room by sneaking out of the window rails. He was a born Houdini.

And there was the bearded Blade. He was a metallurgist, widely feared as the person who hazed (ragged) freshmen the worst.

Everyone is unique.

******

It was on my second week at IIT that Blade and his buddies rounded up a few "*freshies*" to have some fun; I was one of the three chosen. I could hear them coming and knocking on other's doors asking others to come out.

It gave me an inkling of how the Jews must have felt when the Nazis came knocking at their doors.

The hazing session turned out to be not that bad – they just asked us to sing songs and made fun of the obvious fact that we were not as good as Kenny Rogers.

Our set of freshies was an interesting bunch.

Muggo – whose best friends were lifeless books.

Ram – the handsome, rich, blue-eyed one.

Flask – with a deeper voice than most men would like to have.

The *Tamil* gang (The Sambars), the *Telugus* (The Golts), and the *Malayalees* (The Thons).

Gondax – who behaved strangely and was attracted to trouble.

Hash – the friendly Kuwaiti with fancy calculators and awesome technological devices.

Stash – the one who got water airlifted from Hyderabad – and still got jaundice.

Binu – the soccer defender who *thought* he could stop Maradona.

Ramesan – the soccer forward who thought he *was* Maradona.

Cheenbhai – soccer defender who could *possibly* stop Maradona.

Vithy – soccer forward who could *actually* play like Maradona.

Pyari – who knew too much and talked too much.

Saaju – who wanted to be a true disciple of Jesus Christ.

Subra – who saved another Joseph.

Ramaswamy – who had more buttons on his shirt than Michael Jackson.

Sundy – the quiet one, who would have been beautiful if he was a girl.

The other Sundy – the cool, easy-going one.

Hauroon – pure fun.

Karim – the tall skinny one.

Conan – the one who believed that God was everywhere, even in the electric fuse box and the bathroom mirror.

Bala – the leaner one.

Irinyax – the confused one.

Srini – the dream walking day-scholar.

Anu – the only girl.

Shank – the studious day-scholar.

Sriram – the cool day-scholar.

PQ – the gentle one.

Peeta – second only to Muggo.

And I was nick-named Josie, by Somasundaram, the General Secretary of IIT.

It is odd that once you get a nickname, it sticks.

You cannot change it…ever.

Your best hope is that you do not end up with a suggestive nickname that you would not want your sister to ever know.

Joseph Pally

Tell others a good nickname for yourself, before they give you one.

******

CHAPTER 28
FESTIVAL OF LIGHTS

Suresh was so scary that no one dared to give him a nickname. He was Aero's buddy. He was the one who had locked Aero up.

It was *Diwali* – the festival of lights and fireworks.

It was afternoon and everyone was looking forward to that evening. Except Ram – the restless one.

He sent a rocket, up into the sky right around 2 pm.

But the rocket took a turn, zipped across the field, zoomed into a room with an open door and exploded right underneath the steel bed that Suresh was sleeping peacefully on.

Everyone else who was at their siesta also woke up – from the steady stream of four letter screams. Ram said "Sorry," and laughed hysterically.

Suresh had determined that Ram was certifiably and totally mad. Ram had the insanity defense.

When you make a mistake, the best thing you can do is have a good laugh at it.

******

We did strange things to each other during *Diwali*, such as attempted murders with missiles that would have shamed actual murderers.

Pyari, Saaju and I hatched a plan to lower lit bombs from an upper floor, just behind some folks in the floor underneath, who were having an academic group discussion.

The plan misfired.

The bombs exploded as soon as we lit them.

For a moment, we were all deaf.

Then Pyari started moving his lips – as if he was saying something. For a moment, we all thought we had gone deaf.

His lips were moving for a while, but we could hear nothing. We really thought we had gone deaf.

Then we overheard the folks below laughing, and Pyari's lips were still moving as if he was saying something.

We had not actually turned deaf! It was Pyari playing a trick on the rest of us!

Some are deaf, even if they can hear. Some are dumb, even if they can speak. Some are blind, even if they can see. Some are stupid, even if they have all the senses.

******

Diwali at the hostel was always so much fun.

103

Especially with Muggo, who studied 24 hours a day.

It was fun to put lit bombs on his door, knock and run away. He too eventually understood the need for fun and joined in our laughter.

Muggo was a special target of mine.

I remember hiding in the shadows that evening, laying a rocket flat on the ground, and lighting it just in time, when Muggo was halfway across the corridor. I could see a curious, fearful look on his face, which turned redder at the approaching fiery missile.

It came within a few feet of him and exploded with a deafening bang.

That was the only time I saw Muggo scream. We are still friends.

When faced with death, scream and let go. Think that nothing will happen, if you are not already dead. And if you are dead, you won't have time to think.

******

CHAPTER 29
6-6-6

Gondax was the most interesting.

Nature had gifted him with stubbornness, extreme intelligence, strange arrogance and a certain lack of coordination.

He insisted that everyone pronounce his strange last name accurately – with all the vowels of a certain length.

We all had to have a bicycle to get around, everyone except Ram, who had a car. So we all had shipped our bicycles to the hostel.

When Gondax received his bike, he attempted to show off his skills – and the bike kept swerving to the left...more left... and more... until the bike and its rider were on the ground.

Try not to show off. Train before you show off your stunts.

******

"The Omen" was still a popular horror movie back then. We were going to have the movie at the Open

Air Theater that weekend. Me being a Catholic, the movie had more meaning for me than for others. Gondax and I were chatting about the movie that evening at the library.

I wished we had chosen an academic topic as we went, down the dark stairwell. Eerie, it was.

The time was exactly six minutes past six o'clock.

I still do not know why he chose to reveal his big secret then.

He mentioned that he was born on June 6, 1966.

"Six… Six… Six…" he hissed.

His face looked pale, and eyes looked intense.

I froze.

I gulped.

I was faster than Carl Lewis getting out of the stairwell.

If you meet the Anti-Christ, run. It makes no sense to stick around.

******

I kept my distance from Gondax after six in the evening from then on. But it was on another night that I realized he was human after all.

It was the night that he and a deer attempted to avoid each other – but fate would not let them.

Gondax and deer were both hurt. His bike was okay.

People came running. Everyone was trying to help the deer but no one seemed to care about Gondax.

He was human after all.

When you fall, get up.

******

CHAPTER 30
FATE ALMOST

Rains came often to Madras.

Cyclones came once a year. They brought winds so strong that you could not even walk against them. For days you would hunker down. If you kept your windows open, they could slam shut and break the glass.

We slept late in the hostels.

Sometimes we missed nights, so we slept the next day.

Hours were spent debating world affairs at the Nair's chai-shop (called *Tarams*) just outside the campus.

It was after one of those rains that we decided to go to the teashop.

It was one in the morning.

Trees kept the rain alive.

I saw something move under the bluish, dim streetlight. There was something moving next to my feet.

The sting was riveting and the pain intense.

I saw the scorpion with its tail up, injecting venom into my body.

Ramesan once said that scorpions in southern India are not venomous.

Do not take advice from folks who act as if they know everything. Try to know it yourself. Or go to Google.

******

Even if it was painful, I went ahead to the teashop and had the chai – limping all the way.

We met Srini on the way.

As soon as he heard about the scorpion, he made a tourniquet, and started acting like I was going to die. He demanded I go to the hospital at once.

I was taken aback by the speed at which things moved then on. I was in the IIT Hospital within minutes.

It was Dr. Subs. I explained what had happened. He got up, gave me a painkiller, and told me, "Go to sleep. If you get up in the morning, it will be okay."

"What happens if I don't?" I inquired.

"Well," he said, followed by nothing.

Dr. Subs was the same doctor who had mentioned to my friend, "You have jaundice. But you may want to check with the doctor next door to make sure."

If you are faced with death, go to sleep. If you wake up the next morning, you will be okay. Just remember Dr. Subs when you do.

******

"Let us go to *Tarams* for a tea," Sunil suggested.

We were on two bikes and were both pedaling fast.

Suddenly he stopped. I braked.

"Snake!" he screamed.

"Where?" I asked.

"Under your bicycle," he said.

Just under my feet was a snake, about four feet long. I had stopped on top of a snake and by now I had hurt it.

"Oh my God," I screamed, lifting both my feet off the ground.

I fell on top of the snake and the bike.

I would have been killed that day, had the snake been poisonous or otherwise vicious.

The snake was trying to escape, but my bike was over it.

I am not sure how exactly we got out of that mess.

Sometimes there is not a lot you can do, except hope for the best.

******

111

CHAPTER 31
GOOD SHOT

The National Cadet Corps (NCC) was the group to join to learn leadership, service and excellence.

The NCC was different from any other group we could join.

You got guns to shoot.

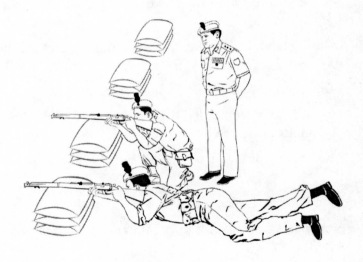

The shooting range was cool.

When an instructor told you do something, it was best to do so.

One time, Amit's rifle stopped firing. It was stuck.

The gun was loaded but it would not fire.

"Look sir, this gun is not firing... Can you see? Nothing is coming out of this thing..." Amit said, pressing the trigger many times to demonstrate, with the barrel pointing in the general direction of the instructor.

I saw the instructor fall to his knees, then prostrate on to the ground immediately – kind of flapping around, screaming "Stop! Do not touch the trigger! Point it away! Please! No, not at others either!"

Teaching can be a deadly job. The first thing you should teach is what not to do.

******

CHAPTER 32
MAD PEOPLE WITH WATER

At IIT hostels, when you became a senior in school, you were given rooms on the upper floors. This meant that it was a constant ritual to fetch drinking water from the water fountain downstairs to your rooms upstairs.

Manoj asked Aji if he could also get him some water when he went downstairs. They had a strange antagonistic relationship, but Aji agreed. Aji never refused to bring water for Manoj whenever Manoj requested.

Manoj, however, did not return the favor when Aji asked him to bring some water.

Aji was angry. He said nothing and kept quiet for a few hours.

"Bang!" We heard the noise, followed by an "Ouch."

Aji had gone down to fetch his own water, came back upstairs, and had banged the glass bottle full of water on Manoj's forehead.

Manoj's blood dripped all over the floor and he was taken to the hospital.

Get your own water.

******

It was 7 pm, and I was on my way back to the hostel mess, when I met Vithy.

He was fetching water in a flask for himself.

"Can I have some?" I asked, "I am very thirsty."

"Absolutely," he said.

And I opened his flask, and poured the water right into my mouth.

I screamed with pain. The flask contained hot water. My throat and mouth had been scalded.

Be specific about what you want. And still you may not get what you want.

******

The water cooler at the canteen attracted all residents of the hostel, like a watering hole.

We would go there to fill our bottles and to drink the cold water straight out of the tap.

Joseph, the mess boy, was taking his fill.

The floor was wet.

And he could not take his hands away from the steel pipe.

We saw his face. Frozen like a tableau, without expression. Just frozen.

The water cooler and the wet floor were electrocuting him.

We could not reach him. Water was around him. I thought of running toward him and pushing him down.

That would possibly electrocute me too, putting two lives in danger.

None of us knew what to do.

Subra was behind me.

He saw the scene and he spotted a wooden chair at the back of the canteen.

He ran and got the chair with his bare hands.

"Everybody move back," he shouted, taking charge of the situation.

He used the dry wooden chair to push little Joseph away from the water cooler. Joseph fell to the ground, away from the wet floor.

Subra had shown such presence of mind, and he saved a life.

Learn how to handle emergencies ahead of time.

******

CHAPTER 33
WEIGHTS AND
MEASURES

"I think you have chicken pox," Dr. Subbs said.

There was a blister-like pustule on my tummy and my family had had chicken pox during my vacation from school.

I decided to head back home. The trip was hell; I remember fainting once due to high fever.

I lost ten pounds by the time I came back to rejoin the school.

I really wanted to gain back the lost weight, so I started eating a lot.

One day, I was at the concrete lab where we had to carry small cubes of concrete to conduct different tests.

I noticed a weighing machine in the lab. I got onto it, and it showed I had gained back all my lost weight.

I was so happy.

After a few days I passed by the same weighing machine, and I decided to check my weight again.

I had lost ten pounds!

It took me another week to figure out what had happened.

The first time I noticed the weight gain, I was holding those concrete cubes in my hand – and I had forgotten to put them down while getting on the scale.

Nothing good happens that fast – especially with body weight!

******

I was not the fastest runner among those taking part in the long-distance race.

"If you run any slower, you will soon be running backwards," someone commented.

"Maybe that is why he looks red in the face," said another.

I knew he was referring to red-shift, which occurred when an object moved away from an observer because of the Doppler effect.

Ignore sarcastic comments. Win the big race of life. Little insignificant races do not matter.

******

I was lost. I could not find the building where one of my lab sessions was going to be conducted.

"How far is the Applied Chemistry Lab?" I asked Chakra.

"Oh, about forty thousand kilometers," he said.

"What?" I asked, surprised.

"But if you turn around and go the other way, it is only a 100 meters that way," he continued.

I remembered that the circumference of the Earth was around forty thousand kilometers.

Direction matters as much as speed.

******

CHAPTER 34
FLASK

Flask had a deep voice and the looks of Sylvester Stallone in the movie *Rocky*.

At least, that is how he thought of himself.

He did not carry a machine gun, but he sure knew he could if he wanted to.

He adored Rocky. The way Rocky climbed over cliffs. The way Rocky drove the cars.

Everything was Rocky for Flask.

It was a strange night. It was 3 am. Flask was in the hallway that held his second floor room. He was alone.

He was just walking across the hallway half-asleep when he saw the dog – a big black one.

A dog on the second floor of a men's hostel was very unusual.

Fear gripped Flask.

It was a narrow hallway with closed rooms on one side and empty space on the other.

Flask had no choice.

The dog ran towards him.

Flask jumped into the parapet, and twisted in the air. He was hanging on one side of that parapet. Just like Rocky – hanging to a cliff.

His grips loosened. The dog was on the other side.

And Flask fell to the ground, from the second floor.

Flask landed on a tree stump, cut by the gardener the day before.

The scream was deafening. People woke up from their dreams. Nobody could figure out what had happened. The night was dark.

Someone saw Flask on the ground, way below. It was a terrifying sight.

Everyone sprang into action.

Ram took him to the hospital in his car. Along with Hash, PQ and many others.

Unfortunately, Flask had landed on the tree stump, right on the head.

It took Flask months to recover, and years to be fully back.

But he fully recovered. He was very strong in mind, will and spirit.

And he still is one of the best people to know.

Difficult events make people strong and pure.

******

CHAPTER 35
THE BOMB

We always looked forward to the Saturday movies at the Open Air Theater (OAT). The Film Secretary chose what movie to show, and this time it was the horror movie – Friday, the 13th.

The city had been shocked by terror attacks – attributed to Tamil Tigers of Sri Lanka. The airport had been bombed recently.

The OAT was full of people watching the movie in the open air. The crowd was terrified by the horror on screen.

I happened to be sitting in front of a large group of girls.

I saw many of the girls getting up from their seats, squealing, but they eventually settled back down. The movie had everybody on edge.

Then, someone behind me screamed.

Something hit me from behind.

"Bomb," someone shouted.

I got up, and in a deft move, ran like a gazelle, jumped over the railing, into the ramp, to get out of the theatre – before the bomb went off.

I was the only one who had run out at that precise moment in time because the object had hit only me. Out of the thousands of people at the OAT, just one had run out.

My reaction time was just faster. Maybe only I was thinking about the Tamil Tigers at that precise moment in time.

It was not a bomb. Someone had thrown a balloon filled with water.

The giggles of those girls when I returned to my seat were more horrifying than the movie.

React swiftly in danger. You may not be right all the time. It is probably okay to look stupid, instead of dead.

******

CHAPTER 36
STARS AND SPOTS

I loved stars. They are always there at night, just looking at us, moving slowly across the sky.

Halley's Comet was approaching the earth. I was so excited to witness something that happened only once every 75 years, so I joined the Astronomy Club.

It was amazing to observe the rings of Saturn, moons of Jupiter, the red Mars, the beautiful Venus and our own pockmarked moon. Orion, the Hunter. Taurus, the Bull. The Big Dipper. The constellations became alive at night.

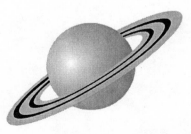

I enjoyed spotting binary stars, star clusters and the nebulas. The 10-cm telescope had become my window to a universe I had never before seen.

It was inspiring to watch the hazy Halley's Comet as it got closer to Earth. I wondered about the life of a lonely comet, as it traversed the dark cold space.

The cold nights spent on the eighth floor of IIT Administrative Building, where the telescope was housed, were some of my most memorable.

But I wanted to see one thing I had not seen so far: sunspots.

I arranged to get the keys to the astronomy club room one afternoon, and went to the top of the building. Unfortunately, the keys to the room didn't work and I couldn't get the telescope out to look at the sun.

I learned a few days later that you must use the solar filter while looking at the sun. If not, the light collected by the large telescope, which is then focused onto your eye, would instantly blind you.

I had not planned to use the filter the day I had gone up to the telescope room to look at the sunspots. I would have certainly blinded myself.

I still do not know why the key did not work. Something made me not to try hard enough to open that lock, I think.

But I was lucky it did not open.

Try to always read the full manual before you use any equipment. You may not always be that lucky.

******

CHAPTER 37
MICHAEL AND
JELLO

Two more days left to enter the art competition, the notice read. Winning could get you as much as Rs. 150.

I knew I could paint well. It would be nice to win the competition, I thought.

Entering was easy. I just had to go to the common room, get the canvas sheet, the colors, and paint whatever I liked and submit it.

I imagined I would do something world-changing. A painting that someday might adorn the rooms of presidents, prime ministers and heads-of-state. A painting that would prick their conscience, if they were to make a rash decision.

That night I painted a mushroom cloud – rose, red, yellow and white – over a blue-green earth, on a deep black background. With the words, 'OH MOTHER' – each letter a tiny circle designed like a little earth, with the letter cut out of each tiny earth.

Many said good things about my painting. That day I imagined that I had made something that could influence the world with its message.

The deadline was noon, the next day. I turned my painting in at 11:55 am.

As I was turning my painting in, Pyari walked in.

Just five minutes to go.

"Where do I sign-up?" he asked the organizing official in the room.

Everyone looked at him in amazement.

"Sign here. You can collect the canvas and paint from the next desk," the official told Pyari.

Just four minutes to go.

Pyari took the canvas sheet, and the paints to a corner. He laid the sheet on the ground. And poured all the paint onto the canvas. He then folded the sheet with all the paint inside, and crumpled up the sheet mixing the paint inside.

Just three minutes to go.

And he named his work of art as "Metamorphosis." Then he submitted it to the official with two minutes to spare.

That evening the results came.

Pyari's "Metamorphosis" was awarded the first place.

His work of total nonsense had gotten the first place. A judge explained his reasons for selecting "Metamorphosis" as a reflection of human mind on paper and vivid colors – celebrating life.

Life does not make sense. Even on paper.

******

CHAPTER 38
MISS. TAKEN

"Do you want to come with us to see a girl?" my cousin asked. He and some family members were going to a girl's home to see if they might be a good match.

Arranged marriages in India were the norm then.

I joined in.

It was my first experience with such an arrangement. Prominent members of the two families meet and try to hype up the greatness of their side. They mentioned their amount of property, and listed the successful and rich members of their respective families.

Prominently avoided was mention of the mentally sick, poor and crazy family members.

The ceremony was formal. Generally, men met in the front room and women met each other inside the kitchen.

I noticed a few women chatting behind the window screen, just behind me.

They were describing how tall the boy was, and how great a match the couple would make. I could overhear their giggles and small talk, teasing the girl.

In these ceremonies, the girl would come out holding tea and other eatables in a tray. She would demurely look up at the 'would-be' husband, and assess whether she would even give him a second look.

The girl came in, and I was the first to be served. I took the cup of tea, and she smiled nicely at me. I returned the smile.

She served tea for everyone and walked back into her room.

The verdict came shortly. She liked the boy.

Families got to action.

They poked each other for more information on the other side, now that the girl had said it was okay.

The marriage between the two was arranged that day.

Later that evening the girl asked if it was okay to talk to the boy, my cousin, now that the families were serious.

Families approved.

And my cousin walked into the room where the girl was to talk to him. "You!" she exclaimed, "I liked that tall guy in the blue shirt, not you!"

That would have been me. Unfortunately, she had assumed that I was the one she was going to marry.

My cousin never called me again.

Look as ugly as possible if you are accompanying someone who is trying to get married.

******

CHAPTER 39
THE GREATEST BOSS

After graduating from IIT, my first job took me to the bustling city of Hyderabad. The day I left my posting at Hyderabad to move to Bangalore, my Jeep driver Sultan told me something surprising, with tears in his eyes.

"You are the greatest boss I have ever had," he said.

I didn't know why he felt that way, and I knew he'd served for over 20 years.

I was not even his boss. I was just one of the folks he ferried across the big city of Hyderabad.

I thought it was possibly because of the accident the Jeep had had with a white car one morning, a year ago.

An officer drove the car, and he must have been a high officer of some sort, evidenced by his air; he was a fat, fair man with white hair and wore a white dress from head to toe.

He was white all over and he reminded me of a polar bear, without the black nose.

I was the only passenger in Sultan's Jeep. Sultan is one of the safest drivers I have ever seen. As a decent and devout Muslim, he had been fasting as a part of his Ramadan ritual.

Sultan was negotiating a roundabout, very safely. Suddenly, the white car came from one side, got right on our side and hit us.

The fat-fair-bear-with-an-air got out of the car. "I will make you pay for this," he screamed at Sultan.

Might is right in a class-based society. The tougher guy with higher social standing wins the fight.

Sultan was silent.

The fat-fair-bear-with-an-air threatened Sultan with severe punishment. He threatened Sultan that he would be taken to the police station.

I got out of the Jeep.

I screamed at the fat-fair-bear-with-an-air so badly that he was quiet for a while.

I could not stand a diffident person like Sultan being stripped down by a guy with an ego. I was an officer too – though just a trainee at that time.

Maybe the fat-fair-bear-with-an-air had not seen me in the passenger seat.

I stood towering over him and pounced on him with my arguments.

"To hell with you," I said. "This is my Jeep. I am going to my office. Do not even think of touching my driver. If you cannot drive properly, go yourself and take some lessons. Do not dare to blame my driver."

At that time another one of our senior officers came by in another car. He joined in the conversation. The big fat-fair-bear-with-an-air had been brought down to earth by now. He admitted his fault, and paid for our damages.

Maybe my defense of Sultan led him to say such kind words.

In any case, I have learned that loyalty is the greatest thing that someone can give you. Loyalty comes not by you demanding it; in fact, you can never demand loyalty.

Loyalty comes purely because you deserve it from someone else.

Be worthy of loyalty. Defend weaker people. Fear no one.

******

If you want to pick up a fight, attack people stronger than you. Wait for the weak to become strong before you attack them. Anything less is not honorable.

The deadly King Cobra is shy and avoids confrontation, unless provoked.

A barking dog seldom bites.

Once you start a fight, do not stop until you win. The victory is sweeter when the fight is fiercer.

******

CHAPTER 40
TYING THE KNOT

Tying the *thali* is the most important aspect of an Indian wedding, as the locket signifies endless love. Even the way the knot is made is significant.

"Three knots. Take this end, put it over the other, twist it around, under the other end, and you are done with the first," said my aunt Rita. She was teaching me how to tie the knot – the official way.

"If you break the thread while tying the knot, your bride would certainly die very quickly," she added, quoting the local beliefs. "And obviously your bride's family may not be too happy with it, as you can understand," she warned.

It was the knot tying time. My bride was ready. Her sister lifted the veil from her neck. The *thali,* set already in its thread, was placed on her neck to be tied by the bridegroom – me.

I noticed that she looked beautiful. Almost like an angel. Her eyes were cast down – she looked shy and demure – and so full of grace.

I was finally going to marry this angel. I was lost in my thoughts, counting my blessings.

"You may tie the knot," the priests said to me.

We had three priests presiding over our wedding. Several thousand were present at the church for the auspicious occasion – many had come even uninvited from faraway places. Friends and family of all shades, colors, backgrounds. Rich. Poor. Christian. Hindu. Muslim.

All were at the church to witness the moment.

I started with the knot. I took the left end, and passed the thread over the right end.

I took the right end over the left end.

I tried to bring the ends back together.

The lights were shining on my bride's neck. Video cameras were rolling, three or four at once. So many cameras were flashing. All focused on this moment. The defining moment.

And the knot was getting more complicated.

I hated systematic anything. I hated learning by rote. I hated the step-by-step, regular everything.

The knot had become very complicated.

I remembered the warning from Aunt Rita, "If the thread gets broken, your bride would die quickly."

The knot was not a knot. It was a mess.

I started sweating, remembering the consequences. I wished I could think of the sequence of tying the knot instead.

Cameras were rolling. Flashes going off all over.

I could not figure out the knot. There were no ends to the knot.

If I left it like that, the *thali* would possibly fall off a little later. That would be embarrassing.

Or if I tried to pull it apart, and restart, that would be laughable.

I now realized how important it was to learn this step-by-step. I was just on the first would-be knot and it was a total mess. I still had to do two more after this one.

My bride was waiting to get married to me and my mind was still totally blank as to how to make this knot.

I remembered how I had taught myself the fourth phase of how to ride a bicycle. I had learned it out of sheer fear.

But this wasn't fear. This was total embarrassment.

Not just for that moment. The cameras had been capturing every millisecond of this total mess. This was permanent – captured forever.

They would have it on video, and it would be studied by generations. "*How Knot To*" – I even named the potential future training video in my mind.

Starring a guy who knew not how to tie a knot.

And a beautiful angel waiting to be married.

The marriage never took place because the guy did not know how to tie the knot.

I looked around. I looked for Aunt Rita.

I tried to tell her with my eyes that I was totally clueless on how to tie the knot.

"Could you tie this knot for me?" I started to ask her.

Then I realized that it was not her job. I was the one who was marrying the bride. If anyone else tied the knot, my bride would be his or her wife.

I was sweating – not because it was very warm at the church, though yes, it was that too.

141

But the knot was a disaster.

I tried to get closer to figure out how to connect the knots.

They thought I was going to kiss the bride – on her neck. That is not allowed until you tie the knot.

I looked up at the roof of the church to ask God, "Why me? Why did this have to happen now?" Some took it as my prayer for blessings from heaven.

For all the high-class education I had received, how could they have never taught me how to tie the knot? Granted, it was a strange knot – but it was not supposed to end up like this.

I had no clue what to do.

I remembered how I learned to ride a bike, again.

Drain on one side, truck on the other. I closed my eyes and in an instant learned how to ride a bike.

I thought to myself. Why was it necessary to tie a knot? Could they not devise a better way to marry? Like how the mice belled the cat? We could think of a knot, already made, hung from the ceiling, and the bride would just put her head inside the knot and it could be done.

But that may look like a noose. The optics would look bad.

Why not invent a *thali* thread with a snap-on knot?

Well, that may not work well. The knot was made difficult to untie, so that the marriage would not break.

Ideas stormed in my head.

I sweated more. I was not making any progress.

Then I remembered a scene from a martial arts movie where the opponent had thrown sand on the fighter's face. The fighter was blinded.

So he closed his eyes. He fought the rest of the fight from memory, and won. Like a crane.

My mind was blank. Maybe my hands could figure it out.

I took the two sides of the thread. I closed my eyes. And I just pulled the thread.

I had no idea why I had pulled so hard. I wanted to get this mess untied, so that I could try again to marry my dream girl.

Or maybe break this thread and get a new thread and start over again. That may not be allowed, once the thread was broken – but I could possibly negotiate that with the church.

I waited for the *thali* to fall off.

The heavens had wanted the marriage to take place, I think.

The knot had been made exactly as I had ever seen, and ever hoped to see.

143

By total, sheer luck. It was a one-in-a-billion chance.

The knot was perfect. Aunt Rita looked at me with pride.

The cameras did not notice the difference. They were focused on the neck of the bride and not on my face, thankfully.

The cameras captured the moments, the details of the fascinating knot made out of sheer accident.

My bride was very lucky, I think. She did not have to die quickly.

I had closed my eyes, and I had learned to tie the knot.

Learn how to tie a knot. Join the Boy Scouts or some other group that teaches you know to tie a knot! Just do it! Before it is too late!!!

******

CHAPTER 41
FLIGHT TO A NEW WORLD

Going to a land far away is an experience for anyone.

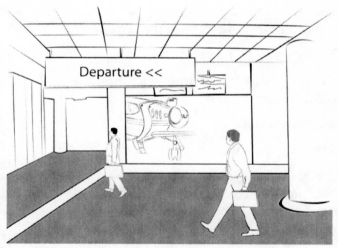

Especially when you are going to the land of opportunity with just $100 in travelers checks in your pocket and only three bags, plus pickles and snacks that your family has packed to make the transition to another world less difficult.

It was my first time in an airplane, a Boeing 747 with British Airways emblem proudly emblazoned on its tail. I found the seatbelt, and figured out how to use it.

I watched the stewardess instruct us on how to use the floatation devices and oxygen masks. I hoped we would never have to use either of them. In any case, I went through the whole safety manual as instructed – just in case.

The plane ride was nice.

I could see mountains and lakes below from my window seat. We passed many nations. But strangely, I saw no boundaries among them from 30000 feet.

Turkey. Jordan. Poland.

Places I had only heard of were passing me by in a real-time map display.

London was nice.

Heathrow matched what I had heard about it.

The view from the transit bus to Gatwick was filled with picture-perfect plains and cute British cottages with deep reddish brown panels and bold white borders.

******

Gatwick was much smaller. My ticket to Houston from Gatwick had been cancelled.

By someone that I did not even know. No one knew what had happened.

"Must be a computer glitch," the lady said. I noticed that she had violet eyelashes and silver eyelids.

"I will have to get you a seat in the smoking cabin, is that okay?" she asked.

"Do I have a choice?" I queried.

"No," she stated.

My trip to Houston was smoky. I sat at the tail of the plane, where all smokers had been quarantined. The girl next to me was a chain smoker.

Houston was a welcoming place. Bright. Not crowded at all like the cities I was used to.

I looked for a luggage cart to carry my three bags. The bags were as heavy as rocks.

Carts are not free in Houston. It was a dollar per cart, or Rs. 40. That was way too expensive for someone with just $100 in hand to survive the next month.

To top it off, I had no coins on me, only travelers' checks.

So I carried three large suitcases. It was hard. Eventually, I started pushing the suitcases along the floor.

I had been advised to avoid going to downtown Houston with a lot of luggage – especially at night, so a friend had agreed to pick me up at the airport and drive me to College Station.

I waited for an unknown friend who never turned up. After six hours, I realized I would have to spend the night at the airport.

Taxis wanted hundreds of dollars to take me College Station.

The only choice was to catch the last flight to College Station from Houston. That would cost just $99.

I was left with just $1.

******

I had an idea to call the number I found in the telephone directory in College Station collect and ask them to help me. A kind soul agreed to accept the collect call. I explained the predicament. He agreed to pick me up from the airport and take me to his home.

College Station was a quiet place.

Texas Aggieland, the welcome sign read. The Home of the 12th Man. Gig'em Ags.

I had no idea what it all meant.

It was already very dark.

The kind soul who finally picked me up knew the person who was supposed to have picked me up.

Apparently, he had slept in.

I was dropped at my unknown friend's apartment.

And I had just $1 for the rest of the month.

In minutes I had dozed off. Thanks to jet lag.

Things can always go wrong unexpectedly, but kind souls are everywhere who can ease the pain.

******

CHAPTER 42
THE SINK THING

Getting a married student housing is like graduating to a much bigger apartment. It is a luxury almost, but at a cheap price.

Our sink was broken, clogged from noodles from upstairs apartment.

The repairman was from Mexico. I explained the problem.

"Si," he said.

"What did you see?" I was confused.

"I said *si*," he said, "Si means yes."

"Oh… Okay," I said.

"I understand. What I cannot understand are the Chinese students. They always say the sink is broken," he said.

"And they always point to something else when I get to their home. I can never get the right tools before going in," he continued.

I knew the problem. I had heard some Chinese students saying "sink" for "thing" too.

I explained it to him.

"Oh… Okay," he said.

What you say is not what others hear. What you mean is not what others see.

******

CHAPTER 43
BIKING IN THE RAIN

I was finally going to get a new rented home. I went through the checklist. Electricity. Water. Telephone.

I checked the numbers. The Utility Department required you to take the lease documents to their office before they would connect anything.

Their office was located a good ten miles away.

I collected my documents and a map, borrowed a bike from my friend, and started on my first journey outside the small range of places I was familiar with.

Without a car, it is difficult to know where places are.

******

I set out from home on my bicycle, which was of the mountain bike variety. I got on the wrong side of the road. For someone who had never gotten used to the right side of the road, it is quite difficult.

Cars honked, from the left and then from the right.

I stopped. I needed to get my bearings.

The rain had started. It came down mildly at first, stronger a bit later.

The rain was bogging down my first bicycle ride in a new country.

But I loved the rain.

The homes I was passing by were decorated for Christmas with bright red rainbows hanging on the stark white door panels.

This city, Bryan, had been selected as the third best place to live in the United States.

It looked beautiful. Quaint. Charming.

The rains came down harder. Water flooded the streets and streamed down the gutters.

I was totally wet. I had about an hour to reach my destination.

And to my horror I realized the back tire had been spraying dirty water up onto the back of my shirt.

I tried to look back. My shirt was completely covered with brown mud.

If I did not get the electricity connections in, I may have to wait for weeks to get them.

Fortunately, the Utility Office wasn't very busy when I finally arrived.

I walked in straight and confident.

153

I did not turn at all, for the fear they would see the mud on the back of my shirt.

Once I was done with the paper work, I walked backwards, without turning my back to the folks inside.

They looked at me as if I was trying to act funny.

Things happen. Live with them.

******

CHAPTER 44
GETTING LOST

My family had just joined me from India.

The course load was heavy that spring semester at Texas A&M University. My computer course assignments were due the next Monday and it was already Sunday.

The computer lab I needed to visit was on the basement floor of an unnoticeable building, on a campus with buildings strewn over miles.

The lab work was intense; I was engrossed.

Hours passed and I had to finish a few more problems that were particularly hard. It was probably eight hours before I returned home.

There was a crowd of people at my home. I knew we had not planned to have a party.

"How could you do this?" A friend came up to me and asked. It looked like someone had died.

"Where were you?" asked another.

"What happened?" I asked, very concerned.

155

"The police have been contacted," one said.

"For what?" I asked.

And I noticed my wife – crying. With all my friends surrounding her.

Something terrible must have happened, I thought, panicked.

"We have search parties looking for you all over the university," one friend said. "No one could find you. Since nobody could find you, we contacted the police."

I remembered I had told her I would be back in an hour. So I called the police station to mention that I was back, safely.

Always let someone know where you are.

******

CHAPTER 45
THE RAT

James Hill, our landlord was a huge man, maybe seven feet or taller.

He was a very friendly guy.

I had noticed some rats in our apartment and I complained about this to Mr. Hill.

He ignored it. Not just once, but three times.

Once, he came to the apartment to replace some furniture. And there it was – a dead rat under the sofa.

"Look Mr. Hill, I've told you so many times that there are rats in this apartment. You have been ignoring me and the rats," I said, with anger in my voice.

"No pets allowed," Mr. Hill said, trying to act seriously while hiding a wry smile.

You can get out of any difficult situation, if you are smart enough.

******

CHAPTER 46
ADS

"Buy our CDs for just $99 and get a boom box," the ad said. The boom box was so big that it looked like it would be at least $79 for the boom box alone, I thought. The picture of it covered the whole TV screen.

The set of two CDs contained almost all of the coolest songs I would have wanted.

I was so excited to get them.

I waited for weeks for the big box of CDs and the boom box to arrive.

Finally, the package arrived. It was an inch thick, shaped like a CD cover. The boom box was nowhere to be seen.

They must have made some mistake, I thought.

A small black object fell from the package. It was about an inch tall and wide. It was the boom box.

Never believe what the ads say.

******

CHAPTER 47
WATCHING PLANTS

"Please watch the plants while I am gone," my wife asked me. She was going to India for a visit.

I did.

I watched the plants every day for weeks.

I watched them turn from healthy green to yellow and then to brown.

I wondered if they had gotten sick.

The next time I called her I mentioned that a strange thing was affecting the plants.

"Did you water them?" she asked.

It is not enough to watch the plants grow. You should water them. Likewise, it is not sufficient to watch young children grow. You should nourish their minds with the best.

******

160

CHAPTER 48
THE FIRST
REVOLUTION

It was in the computer science lab that I first heard news of something new. Something called Mosaic.

The guy on my left told the guy on my right about this new thing; it was a software program called an internet browser. They were so excited that they kept

screaming – completely ignoring me.

"This will change everything," one said.

"Imagine what it means," said the other.

"Those guys are crazy," I murmured to myself.

Little did I know how that concept would redefine my life.

The rumbles of a revolution are easy to miss. Keep your ears to the ground.

******

"In two years, everyone will be checking the traffic on the streets through the web before they go somewhere. The World Wide Web will literally change the way we think about traffic." I overheard Tom telling this to a visitor.

Tom was a director at the Texas Transportation Institute. The year was 1994.

"This Houston Traffic Map will be the way they get their traffic information," he continued, showing the visitor a map with the status of traffic on the main freeways of Houston.

It sounded crazy to me.

I knew computers too well to know that it was not a practical application.

How could people on dialup connections even think of downloading such large images?

How could a common person use the web to find traffic information?

I hadn't even seen it coming, and I couldn't even see it coming.

Think beyond where you are; way beyond where you are.

******

CHAPTER 49
CAR TALK

Life in the United States can be difficult without a car.

Having a car is difficult without a driver's license, money, and insurance.

Our family had two bicycles that took us as far as we could go.

We made sure to buy the best locks to protect them. At the university, some folks would steal your bike in a matter of minutes. Some students stole bicycles for fun.

I lost the key to my bicycle lock once, with no way to unlock my bike other than to cut it off of the steel frame – which would have been more expensive than the bicycle itself. The lock was almost as expensive as the bicycle – so strong that only someone with a key could unlock it.

Finally, the university impounded it and cut the lock with gas cutters. I never saw my bicycle again.

Take some risk when it comes to protecting things. Do not overprotect them.

******

My wife and I met Freddy and Suelly – a Seventh Day Adventist couple – through their evangelization efforts. They would sometimes come by our little home to preach their gospels.

I found it interesting to argue with them about God and religion. They had proof that the Pope was the Anti-Christ, which went against my belief that Damien was the Anti-Christ.

They were our best friends in a land with few friends we could count on, so I asked Freddie if he would teach me how to drive.

He did exactly that over the next several Saturdays. He must have felt like he was facing death a few times while I was behind the wheel, yet he had faith in me.

The day I got my drivers' license was as exciting as the day I got my first Citibank credit card. I was free at last to drive wherever I wanted.

With freedom comes responsibility.

******

At a state university, those who owned cars worth $3000 were considered rich. The ones with new cars were fortunate and respected.

165

My glossy blue Nissan Stanza was a good deal for a thousand bucks.

Once I had a car, the first thing I decided to do was to take a trip to the Laundromat. After dropping the clothes off at the laundry, I took a ride in my new car. I loved the lit dashboard and its neon-like green dial markers and bright red pointing arrows. I switched off the car.

I lowered the drivers-side window and listened to the noises of the night.

The chirping of the crickets.

The wind in the trees.

I watched the road ahead in the bright headlights of my car.

I had my first car.

Life was never going to be the same.

I would never have to push the grocery cart all the way to my home in the cold winters and during the hot Texas summers, and then have to push the empty cart all the way back to the store.

I could visit anyone without having to wait on a friend to pick me up.

It must have been about half-an-hour; my clothes would now be ready, so I decided to go back. I noticed that the headlights had somehow lost their intensity.

I tried to start my car. There was no response. The car was dead. My new car, worth a thousand bucks, was dead.

Murphy's law is the rule. Not the exception.

******

And I was stuck on a dark road with a dead car. My clothes were in the laundry and could be stolen if I was not there in time.

I got out of the car. I didn't know what to do, so I decided to walk about a mile to a friend's home. Zahroof knew a few things about cars. His dad used to own a car dealership.

He was kind enough to come and take a look. He said it was just a dead battery. He got his jumper cables and hooked his car to mine, which started my Stanza up again.

He asked me to not leave the lights on and to get a set of jumper cables.

Switch off the lights when you switch off the car.

******

The best way to learn about cars is to buy an old car.

It was my second trip to the Indian grocery store. As soon as I parked, I noticed smoke rising from the car's hood. I got my family out of the car immediately, to safety. I was expecting the thousand-dollar car to go up in flames at any moment.

I went and told the shopkeeper that there was the potential for a fire outside. He came out looking concerned. He said it did not smell like smoke.

He asked me to open the hood of the car. I did so with great care, expecting flames to pop out, but it was a broken pipe with steam puffing out.

"That's easy to fix for now. Just use duct tape," he said.

I bought a complete roll of duct tape to go along with my new jumper cables.

My thousand-dollar car would soon be a well-equipped mobile workshop.

I had also gotten a car-jack lever to protect my car from thieves. The device came with a note saying that the manufacturer would pay one thousand dollars if someone could break in and steal the car.

Later, I was told that you had to prove that the thief had actually broken the car-jack lever, which would possibly be missing if the car had been stolen anyways.

Read the fine print.

******

CHAPTER 50
CAR WASH

After about a month, I noticed that my new, old car looked really dusty and dirty. How did other folks have such good-looking cars when mine was so full of dust?

As the summer wore on, the car got dirtier and worse to look at.

Then came the summer drizzle.

The drizzle did not wash my car. The slight rain was just not strong enough and the car just looked dirtier with muddy spots.

I wanted to find a place to wash the car, but I did not know whom to ask. I had heard of automatic car washes, but I didn't want to spend a lot of money on a machine that I didn't know how to operate.

I was actually worried about entering one of those small rooms with the giant, spinning brushes. What if it broke the windshield glass and sprayed me with the stuff? How would you escape if it went haywire all of a sudden?

One day, I decided to take a trip to the church. I put the car-jack on, locked the doors and went into the church. I rarely go to church on Sundays, but I enjoy going when no one is there. God may be freer at that time.

When I came out, my car looked horrible.

It had been drizzling a bit. A grass cutter had come by and sprayed cut grass all over my car. It was covered with grass all over. Ugly and dirty as hell.

This car needed a wash.

Murphy's Law rules.

******

I drove all the way down Texas Avenue trying to figure out what to do. I had no money with me to try out the automatic car wash. Plus, it would be too embarrassing to ask someone how to operate it.

Then I saw the magical sign.

"Free Car Wash," it said.

There were a bunch of kids waving a free car wash sign.

America is a free country. This is as free as it comes.

Now I knew how people washed their cars. There was a free car wash on Saturdays on Texas Avenue.

I drove in and got in the queue of cars waiting to be washed.

The kids looked a bit taken aback when I drove in for my free car wash.

It was possibly the worst looking car they had seen.

Let me put it this way: no one had ever seen so much grass and dirt on a car.

The kids were so nice. They came all at once. Some washed the wheels. Some cleaned the glass. They worked so hard. They cleaned it with soft clothes.

I got out of the car and checked it out. My car looked like new.

I got into the car. Opened the window. Called the kids closer.

"Thanks so much for the free car wash. You guys are wonderful," I said. And drove off.

I saw the kid's faces on the rear-view mirror. They looked confused and surprised.

I was so happy to have a clean car, after all.

All effort is worth it, whether free or not.

******

I called my friend and told him that I finally got my car cleaned, and told him about the free car wash near Texas Avenue.

"You mean you did not give them anything?" my friend asked.

"It is completely free. The sign said so. The kids were so nice," I said.

"You're supposed to pay them money," he said.

172

"Why? The sign said it was free," I argued.

"They usually do it for a cause, and you need to contribute to the cause. You should pay them ten or twenty dollars," he said.

"How much does an automatic car wash cost?"

"About four to seven dollars," he said.

I felt miserable. I had seen the sign say something about a library. The kids must have been so disappointed at my driving away without paying. My car was the dirtiest, and they would never wash another car without collecting money first from anyone who looked like me.

I immediately went to the bank and took twenty-five dollars out of my account. I drove back to the free car wash place.

It is never too late to right a wrong.

******

This time when I drove into the queue, they were surprised and confused. My car looked like new and did not need a wash.

I rolled down the window and called them closer. None of the kids looked like the ones who had washed my car. They may have given up and left after I drove off without paying.

173

"What is the cause you guys washing cars for?" I asked.

"We are supporting the local library," they said.

"Keep this," I said, giving them two tens and a five dollar bill.

"Thank you so much, sir," the kids said. They still looked confused, as I had paid without receiving a car wash.

They smiled and waved when I left this time.

There is nothing that is really free. You have to pay for everything.

******

CHAPTER 51
PERCEPTION

Until I got my first pair of eyeglasses, I always thought the horizon was a bit hazy. Trees were a bunch of green. Folks just had black patches on their heads rather than hair.

I stepped out of the optometrist's office and my world had completely changed. I felt like I was walking on the moon. My eyes could not adjust to seeing individual leaves on the trees.

My steps could not adjust to the depth of vision I now had. I could see each hair on other people's heads.

I drove down Texas Avenue, which bisected the city of College Station, Texas. I could see for miles ahead.

I went to the mall.

I could see clearly.

It was all a matter of a pair of eyeglasses. Or contact lenses, a few years down the road.

Your perception is your reality, and that may not be the reality at all.

******

175

CHAPTER 52
DRY SYNDROME

It rarely snows in College Station, but when it does, people get into trouble.

Just a slip and I was on the ground. The umbrella handle I held in my one hand had popped out a bone in the palm of my hand.

"You have a fracture," the doctor said. "It may take about four months to heal."

******

"You have chicken-pox," the doctor told my surprised wife. "It will take weeks to recover. It can spread to others, so you may want to remain at home."

"Do not take aspirin, it may cause you to have Dry Syndrome. It is fast and sometimes fatal," the doctor continued. My wife had taken some aspirin a few days before.

******

I couldn't drive, and she couldn't drive either.

After several days, I started noticing that my wife's face was getting dry.

It kept getting worse. I was concerned.

******

I am a certified hypochondriac.

I walked to the library and pulled out all the medical encyclopedias they had.

I looked for Dry Syndrome and wasn't able to find anything.

I did not know what to do. My wife now had just days to live. And with Chicken Pox, no one was going to drive us to the hospital.

I was growing more and more concerned. I started preparing for her death. I was extra nice to her.

******

I went back to the library that afternoon. I was frustrated that I could not find any information on Dry Syndrome.

Then I read about aspirin, and I read that it could cause Reyes Syndrome.

I read more about it.

My wife certainly did not have Reyes Syndrome. She just had dry skin.

Sometimes the less you know, the better.

******

177

CHAPTER 53
QUACK

Sunny, my father-in-law, wanted to be a doctor.

He couldn't be one, but he imagined that he could easily have been one.

I was visiting India by myself.

I had a sugarcane juice one day from a street vendor. I noticed that the vendor was reusing drinking straws after I had finished my glass of juice.

That didn't look too good.

Soon I was sick. I had fever, severe diarrhea and a severe stomachache. And I was vomiting.

"Feed a cold and starve a fever," Sunny advised me.

For the first time, I thought I would listen to his advice.

I starved the fever; I had nothing at all to drink or eat for the next day. And for another half-day after that.

I wanted to starve the fever. Maybe to lose some weight, if possible. It was a nice time to diet, anyways.

I felt dizzy when I got up in the late evening. I went to the dining table.

"Give me some *kanji* (rice soup) fast," I said.

Then I just fell on the floor. I had fainted.

While falling, I cut my forehead.

There was blood on the floor and on my face. I was unconscious on the floor.

Always have a will ready.

******

Someone sent for a doctor.

Someone called my wife. She was still in the United States.

She picked up the phone.

"Your husband fell unconscious and collapsed on the floor. Pray for him. That is all we can do," the caller said. My wife also fainted from the news – half a world away.

A message may not be the same when it gets to the recipient.

******

I was in bed when I woke up. There were twenty people around me.

"Tell me what happened," said the doctor. I could smell his breath – he certainly was a bit drunk. "What did you have to drink or eat?" the doctor asked.

179

"Nothing for the day," I said.

"You must be dehydrated. Why did you not have anything?" he asked.

"I was starving the fever," I said.

"And you did not drink or eat anything at all?" he asked.

"Sunny told me to do so," I said.

"Who?" he asked.

Sunny had moved to hide behind someone else.

The doctor put a bandage on my forehead.

"You will be okay, just take enough fluids. Do not listen to Sunny anymore," he said.

Partial data is dangerous. Partial information is dangerous. Partial knowledge is dangerous. Partial intelligence is dangerous.

******

I was telling my young cousin what had happened.

"You didn't know that you had to drink fluids to hydrate yourself? Everyone here knows that," she said, laughing at me.

Do not listen to quacks. Especially folks who may have failed to become doctors. Know how to stay hydrated.

******

180

CHAPTER 54
JOHN DOE

Dr. Messer, my thesis advisor, gave me a sample letter to send for my thesis defense.

It would be a pleasure to have you attend the oral examination .... The letter went.

Yours faithfully,

(Your name)

cc.　　Your Graduate Advisor

　　　Your Board

　　　John Doe

I prepared the letter. I changed all the variables in the letter.

Six copies. One to the Graduate Office. One to the Advisor. Two to the two other members. One for myself. Sixth to John Doe.

I started looking for a nameplate in the building for John Doe.

I had a few days to find John Doe; my thesis defense was in one week.

I opened the local Eagle Newspaper the next morning.

John Doe had turned up dead at the hospital.

I broke the sad news to my advisor the next day.

And my advisor started laughing. Hysterically.

"Strange," I thought.

It is okay to make a mistake. It happens to everyone. Well, almost.

******

CHAPTER 55
RAYS OF HOPE

Ray was a friend of a friend. Ray was visiting his friend, Jay.

Jay had bought a nice new table, solid wood with glass on top.

"Do you like it, Ray?" Jay asked.

"Yes, I like it, except the reflection," said Ray.

Like yourself.

******

Ray had a peculiar way of driving. He would stop as soon as he saw a red light, even if the immediate light downstream was green and the red light was way down the street.

It was that Friday night that Ray decided to stop the car behind another, across a railroad track. He was waiting for the queue to clear and it was taking too long, so Ray shut the car off.

The music was loud. I saw a bright light from afar. It looked steady.

It was getting larger.

I thought that could be a train.

"Ray, there's a train coming," I said with concern in my voice.

"Where?" Ray queried, calmly.

"There." I pointed out the train to Ray.

"Okay," said Ray, and he turned the music up louder.

I knew that we had stopped across the tracks.

"Ray, I think we are on the tracks, and the train is approaching – towards us," I said.

He didn't have a clue. I still can't figure out how fast he restarted the car and how fast we cleared the tracks.

But it was real fast. I know that for sure.

The train passed by us with a loud, thundering noise and we had lived to tell the story.

Do not stop over railroad tracks, ever.

******

I remembered the first train I ever saw.

It was a long goods train pulling hundreds of cars.

I started to count the cars but the number exceeded 100, which was the largest number I knew. I thought it was an endless train.

Someone taught me how to know if a train was coming by keeping your ear to the rail. I also learned how to keep a coin on the tracks so that passing trains would flatten it into odd shapes.

I remembered my first trip in a train. I looked out of the window and tiny pieces of coal from the steam engine would fly into my eye.

We traveled in a compartment meant to carry goods once. It was dark. The bogie was packed with people with no windows or lights.

Over time, train tracks changed from meter gauge to broad gauge. The trains grew wider. Diesel engines replaced the dirty but impressive steam engines.

Decades later, electric engines replaced the diesel engines. Trains stopped chugging along the tracks and became silent, gliding worms – connected from front to back.

Charm makes way to progress. Invariably. For better or for worse.

******

CHAPTER 56
THE ELEVENTH HOUR

I had a secret strange phobia. A very strange one.

I never wanted to be in the city of Bombay on the August 11 of any year.

I had never been to Bombay, nor did I expect to go. But I just never wanted to be in that city on that specific date of any year.

Due to a series of coincidences, my ticket back to the United States from one of my visits was on August 11, via Bombay.

I decided not to be superstitious; it didn't make much sense in the twentieth century.

I finally checked in for the flight and the time was 11:30 pm. I felt good that the city of Bombay looked just fine on that day. I felt my strange phobia slipping away. I had another hour before I could board the flight, so I decided to have dinner in a restaurant at the airport.

"The *Chicken Biriyani* (a rice dish mixed with meat) is excellent here, sir," said the waiter.

"Get me one, please," I ordered.

The order arrived.

The time was 11:55 pm.

I was halfway through the dish when I bit something hard, like a rock or piece of metal.

I was gagging with food and a strange object in my mouth. I was gulping the food down while trying to spit out the object.

The time was 11:59 pm.

I tried to hold on until the clock went past midnight, without gulping nor spitting anything. I did not know what I was dealing with, but I wanted to get rid of the jinxed day first.

Finally, I forced out a nail from my mouth, about an inch long, bent in the middle at a right angle.

If I had swallowed it, I could have been in serious trouble. I complained to the restaurant owner about the nail in the food.

"I am sorry, sir, I can get you another plate of *Biriyani*," he offered.

"No way am I going to have any more of that stuff," I responded.

"Please wait, sir," he said, and he gave me the check.

He had only charged half-price for the Chicken *Biriyani*.

Listen to your gut. All irrational fears may happen. Most of the time they do not.

******

CHAPTER 57
CREATIVE
DESTRUCTION

Enron was a very confusing place. "If we say we will do something, we will do it. If we say we won't, we won't," a sign read.

"We treat others as we would like to be treated ourselves ... We do not tolerate abusive or disrespectful treatment. Ruthlessness, callousness and arrogance don't belong here," read another.

"Ask why," read yet another.

The conversation went on in eager sincerity.

"This is one of the most exciting companies in the world," said one Enron employee.

"Enron has never had a layoff," boasted another.

The fact is, if it sounds too good to be true, it probably is.

Enron was a house of cards. I met so many interesting people while working there, some good, some greedy, some awful, and some clever. Some who were just plain smart.

It was not just Enron. Wall Street, the Main Street, the SEC, auditors – they were all part of the collective hysteria.

There is value in the free market system. The most efficient transaction is supposed to be determined by supply and demand.

However, when someone is making $500 million in profits during the energy crisis in California, there was something wrong.

Common sense is not so common.

******

Folks do not learn easily. When things are good, everyone wants in and no one stops to think.

The stock markets crashed in 2008. Not because no one knew, but because no one wanted to know.

When failures occur, lawyers get to their dirty work. Those who were "wronged" act innocent. Those who may have done something wrong oftentimes never realize or admit their part in the disaster.

Internet boom and bust and Mortgage crisis; the house of cards built on risks that were swapped like hot potatoes.

When will financial engineers stop making fools of common men who hardly understand shares and risk? Making something complicated does not make it right; selfish, short-term interests dominate the game.

Greed of many shades: for money, for votes, for power, for things. Work without effort.

When will folks ever learn?

But failures MUST happen. That is the way things become better. Otherwise we would all still be monkeys hanging on trees.

There is a need to fail. Embrace failures as the best teaching moments.

******

CHAPTER 58
PLANNED
WHATEVER

We planned our trip to England carefully. On our way back to Houston, we would take a three-day break in London. Our plan was to leave our luggage at the luggage holding facility at the airport, stay at the Gatwick Inn, and then take the train to London. We would visit Buckingham Palace on day one, Hyde Park on day two and Brighton on day three.

We landed in London, weary from travel, with eight huge pieces of luggage and went directly to the luggage holding facility.

"We have stopped taking any new clients for the day," the lady said. The facility was overbooked. We needed to wait for about six hours for space to free up.

The plans had started to unravel.

It is not fun to move around eight huge pieces of luggage, especially when you are not familiar with where you are going to spend the night.

194

We took two taxis to carry everything to the Gatwick Inn.

"There is only one room left today, sir. It is on the third floor. Is that okay?" asked the innkeeper.

"Okay," I accepted.

"Unfortunately, the elevators have stopped working today," she said.

It was no fun lugging eight pieces of luggage up three flights of stairs.

The pieces of luggage filled up the room so that we had hardly any space to move around.

Expect the worst combination. Yet, things will work out.

* * * * * *

The London bombings had started just before we had landed, and tube stations, buses, etc. had been hit. People were scared and using the tube was a bit unsafe. Actually, nothing was safe.

London was fun, dodging reported bombs and alert people who watched your every move – especially if you carried a backpack.

It seemed as if all young men with beards were carrying backpacks, as if to confuse already-wary people.

We still made it to Hyde Park, the London Eye, the Thames, the Borough Market, Shakespeare's Globe Theatre, the London Bridge and Bakers Street.

We revisited the adventures of Sherlock Holmes and Oliver Twist. We relived the era of kings and queens.

There is charm and horror in the frozen past. Just like the present.

* * * * * *

Brighton – a city south of England – was beautiful.

"Is that the English Channel?" I asked a teenager at the beach.

"I think it is the Pacific Ocean," he confidently said.

I knew that was clearly wrong.

Teenagers should be at school during day. Not at the beach.

******

The day came for us to leave London. The elevator in the hotel was still not working and we had to carry the eight big pieces of luggage all the way down this time.

We left London happy but weary.

Planning needs to account for constant changes. Do not be paranoid about plans. Some will fail. Make things interesting by being creative on the run.

******

CHAPTER 59
ATTITUDE

Great things may occur amid disaster, but it all depends on your attitude.

My friend, Ken Vaughn, used to put it in simple terms: You need to walk before you can run.

And you need to fall before you can walk.

Progress consists of many steps forward and some steps backward.

******

Your attitude determines your altitude. You cannot beat your enemies by casting curses on them.

The best way to get revenge is to rise so far above your enemies that they are left wondering what happened; it is like a slap in the face.

******

I remember 9/11, as most do. It was a disaster that appeared out of nowhere on that clear day. So many died. Yet, we remember the heroic efforts of the many fire fighters and first responders and their selfless work.

It was obviously a day of great disappointment. A day when everything changed; a day never to be forgotten.

A day that led to the complete transformation of the world we knew.

I headed home from work when the second tower collapsed.

In front of me was a truck. It had, "AMER-I-CAN" written on its back.

I noticed the words, "I CAN."

I felt proud of my adopted country – even when she was going through her most difficult time.

You can, only if you believe.

******

CHAPTER 60
ESSENCE OF
EXISTENCE

I have always felt that Christianity is a religion of contradictions. Some say that the essence of Christianity is imbibed in the "Sermon on the Mount".

Meek shall inherit the earth? Love thy enemy? Turn the other cheek?

How does it work?

God knows.

******

The selfless seem to be the content ones, the greedy have the most turbulence in their life. Greed seems to be the mantra of the stupid.

I am yet to see a billionaire who is cherished because he made a lot of money. I can think of many who have shared their money wisely to do good things.

Andrew Carnegie, a quarter-billionaire, is widely known for Carnegie libraries.

Warren Buffet, the frugal multi-billionaire, is known for his giving away of most of his money to the Bill & Melinda Gates Foundation for curing the world's ills.

Bill & Melinda Gates will in the future be known for their philanthropy, not for Bill's role in Microsoft.

There is something to be admired in these visionaries – they use their money to make a difference in this world. They invest in charity, making millions of people happy.

The more you give, the more you get. Both good and bad.

******

Capitalism is best if you see capital as effort.

Money as a number makes you blind to reality. When you look at numbers, you lose your perspective. And that makes greed as your driving force.

When you see capital as one's effort, you optimize the right factors – not numbers. Most folks have problems with numbers.

When Wall Street dealt with straight stocks – and did not confuse itself with 'derivatives' – things were better.

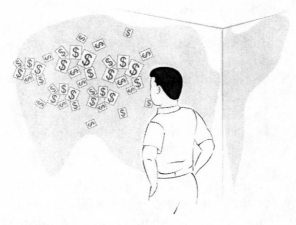

Collective and effective effort is what capitalism should be based on. Not the amount of money.

******

The best you can do is to be prepared against the selfish, yet act selflessly. If it offends your principles, act viciously. Even if you do not need to be, act with consideration.

"Win-Win or No Deal" – a philosophy pushed into the spotlight by Steven Covey in his *Seven Habits of Highly Effective People* – seems to work wonders. This philosophy creates great and enduring human relationships, and culls the ones that are based on greed. When you want other party also to win, you

202

are setting yourself up for long-term relationships that reward tremendously.

Think Win-Win. Never lose.

******

CHAPTER 61
GREED

"Greed is right. Greed works. Greed clarifies, cuts through, and captures the essence of the evolutionary spirit. Greed, in all of its forms -- greed for life, for money, for love, knowledge -- has marked the upward surge of mankind." – Gordon Gekko in *Wall Street*.

I have never seen greed work. Not even once. Try to think of one example where greed eventually made sense. I can find none.

Maybe folks attribute greed to the Darwinian theory of evolution: "The survival of the fittest." Evolution of life is now attributed to symbiosis, where useful characteristics from partners who coexist and share create new life forms. Lynn Margulis proposed and proved that all complex beings are combinations of bacteria in symbiosis and coexistence. Four billions years of life was not a result of random mutations, but a story of sharing.

Stop taking. Start giving.

******

Andrew Grove coined the motto: "Only the Paranoid Survive." Often quoted, it does not match reality. Wikipedia – a computer program based on open source and sharing – killed off similar, only-available-through-purchase programs such as Microsoft Encarta and Encyclopedia Britannica. A free service called Google threatens Microsoft. Tim Berners-Lee's vision of an open World Wide Web trounced Ted Nelson's closed-concept of Xanadu.

Interestingly, Ted Nelson, who coined the term "hypertext", promotes four maxims: Most people are fools, most authority is malignant, God does not exist, and everything is wrong. But if everything is wrong, how about the first three of Ted's maxims?

The converse is actually true. Greed is stupid. Greed is not attractive. Greed does not work. It destroys, kills and stunts growth.

Everything excels and multiplies when shared. Knowledge grows when shared. Love multiplies when shared. Money comes back to you ten-fold when invested wisely. Acts of love bring smiles.

Greed only brings frowns and anger.

******

Yet, greed is something to watch out for. It exists – mostly among the cowardly and the paranoid.

Greed has to be factored into human relationships as it has a tendency to rear its ugly head when things may not be so good. It is always good to know how others may behave under altered circumstances.

Do not tolerate greed in others or yourself. Unless you want to look like an ugly cow.

******

CHAPTER 62
THE NINE THINGS

I came to recognize a set of nine things that make
relationships awesome.

******

16.6.90

To You,

- Your love, as much as you can give.

- Your affection, as much as I need.

- Your care, as much as I want.

- Your concern, as long as we are alive.

- Your corrections, whenever I am wrong.

- Your support, whenever I am right.

- Your attention, as much as I deserve.

- Your intimacy, as far as it is allowed.

- The feeling that I belong to you and you are mine.

Give me all of them with complete sincerity.

I promise the same from myself, and more.

From Me.

******

I know they work.

What these nine things tend to control is greed in all but the most selfless of desires.

Be selfless. You will have everything, and you will need nothing.

******

CHAPTER 63
THE X-FACTOR

Like all good schools in the world, IIT gives you a very supportive alumni network. You meet folks who went through those same doors twenty years before you and twenty years after you.

It was through my alumni network that I learned about the X-factor. Biki introduced me to the concept.

"There are four levels of success in career, guys," he said to a group of us who were listening. "The first is the Technical Level. The second is the Managerial Level. The third is the Executive Level. And the fourth is the Entrepreneurial level. The X-Factor is how much money you make in these levels," he continued.

If you want more people to listen to your ideas, put your ideas in terms of money. A selfish world likes green filters.

I started listening intently. It was getting interesting. I wasn't being introduced to something new; it was that I was being told something in a way that made sense.

"And the skills that you need to jump from the Technical Level to the Managerial Level are very different than your technical skills," he went on.

"It is the car you drive. It is the house you live in. It is how well ironed your shirt is. It is how well you impress people. It is your way of speaking, your accent," he paused to sip some wine.

"And to get to the next level, the Executive Level, the skills you need are entirely different. It is how you lead. It is how you share ideas, money and vision with others. Get involved in voluntary efforts, charities and such. Others notice your actions. They start to follow you. You will then be making ten times the money you used to make as a technical professional," he continued.

The stream of advice was interrupted by laughter from the next table.

"And the next level – of the entrepreneur – involves risk-taking. You may make much money or none at all. You may make zero-X to infinity-X. Given time, you will make a lot."

He rambled on to anyone who would listen.

I was already an entrepreneur with a good consulting business. Biki's advice seemed to make sense.

Perception matters more to the world than reality.

******

CHAPTER 64
JOE, THE PRESENTER

My flight had just landed. I collected my luggage and headed to the tower in Chicago.

My presentation was at 1 pm.

I got out of the taxi, right on time.

"Thirty-fourth floor, ask for Andrew. Everything will be ready," I had been told by the organizer of the meeting.

"Joe?" someone asked me when I stepped into the 34th floor.

"Yup," I said.

"Please come with me," the young man said, "I will take you to the presentation room."

I had lots of presentation material with me. I had to connect the laptop, the projector, organize the connections, and the printouts.

I was shown the room to present in.

I was supposed to meet with a few people to present a software solution. The client was interested.

But this room had lots of space. It was a big room with many chairs.

It was 12:30 pm.

I got everything organized and I started to rehearse my presentation a bit.

People started arriving. The crowd grew. They started munching on their lunches.

Lunch started to wrap up – everyone was ready to attend the presentation.

It was 12:55 pm. I took a seat among the crowd. Just to wait.

I heard them talk about chemical plants. They seemed excited about today's presentation. I had no clue about chemical plants; I was not going to talk about them.

12:59 pm.

A guy in a black suit walked into the room and took a seat close to the lectern. Another person came into the room, ready to introduce the speaker.

"Joe is an expert in the chemical industry," he said. I was not an expert in the chemical industry.

"The chemical industry has been seeing great growth," he continued. I was not prepared to talk about the chemical industry at all.

I got up. The guy in black suit also got up.

We were both confused.

We both were named Joe. This was not my presentation.

I had been taken to the wrong room and had set up for the wrong presentation. I was the wrong person. I just had the right name at the wrong time.

Assume strange coincidences can happen.

******

CHAPTER 65
ARROGANCE

Lupe's Tortillas has the best beef fajitas in Houston. One day, Bryan, who was at the restaurant with two other female officemates, rudely interrupted our lunch there.

A waitress had accidentally toppled a glass of water on the two guests, just by sheer accident.

"You have 'destroyed' our lunch," he screamed. The actual verb was much worse.

The waitress was close to tears, was very apologetic.

Everyone at the restaurant noticed his rudeness and it was clear that he was only interested in impressing the two women.

Later I saw Bryan backing up his car in the parking lot. By mistake, he hit another car that was parked.

That car belonged to the same waitress he had hurt that afternoon.

The waitress came out of the restaurant. A red-faced Bryan tried to explain his mistake.

She coolly responded, "You should be considerate of other's mistakes. It is okay."

Be considerate of other's mistakes. Things have a way of coming back at you.

******

"I want half of all that you own," Dick said. He had just finished drinking a Bloody Mary and had turned from the normal person I knew into a snake.

"Respect all agreements," I said, "or else I will not deal with you."

I make small agreements and I keep them. I expect others to fully abide by their word.

What he needed was a shrink, not a drink. I decided never to deal with this snake again. I left him to go back to whatever hole he had crept out of.

Sometimes people want to be bad – out of insecurity and fear.

Sometimes they become irrational – out of arrogance.

Sometimes they become strange – out of stupidity.

Some become all of the above.

All evil starts between your ears.

Everyone deserves a chance – only when they shed their arrogant skin. A real man keeps his promises in any and all circumstances.

******

215

CHAPTER 66
TAKING CARE WELL

Kevin loved cars, especially yellow racing cars.

He had just joined the company and he had just married his girlfriend.

And he had just heard about the new special edition Honda that was coming out. There were only forty being released worldwide.

Kevin got one.

He loved his new car. He loved it so much that he even joined a newsgroup for that specific make of car.

There were only a few such cars in Houston, six, at the most.

It was a special car.

It was the apple of his eye, until it was stolen.

The car was later found. Well, just the shell. The rest was gone.

Anything made by man, can be taken apart.

******

Kevin used his insurance money to buy a new Yellow Honda.

Kevin loved his new car even more than he had loved the last car.

He wanted to protect it, so he installed a top-of-the-line burglar-proof mechanism. The car would auto-disable if it were ever stolen.

He saved some money getting the car fixed up by a moonlighting employee of the car company.

Kevin felt strange when he had to leave the car at the airport to go on a long trip.

When he came back, he had forgotten the magic code to the car.

He opened the car door, but the car needed the code to work.

In minutes the car was disabled.

Kevin's car would not start again.

Kevin called the company that had sold him the alarm.

They said they could not support it, since the company had not installed it.

Kevin could not get the car enabled again.

Protect not as much as it destroys what you protect.

******

CHAPTER 67
UNBREAKABLE
GLASS

I hate shopping, unless it is for an expensive car, electronics or computers. I hate buying clothes. I go shopping for clothes only once every two years and get everything for the next few years within a span of two hours. I would then only unpack them whenever there was nothing else to wear.

But when your family is leaving for India to visit their relatives, you need to shop.

Fortunately, Indians drive on the wrong side of the road. So you do not have to buy a car to bring to your family. Unfortunately, India uses a bizarre 220V electrical system that makes any electronics you can get from the United States incompatible.

So I went looking to buy something that would be useful for our friends and family back home.

Electronics and More in Houston looked interesting; there were so many cool things to buy. Fancy stuff. Some gaudy.

I asked for some vases or glass cups.

"Sir, I have something 'especial' for you," the shopkeeper said.

"What is it?" I asked.

"I have something new. Made in Italy. Set of nine glass cups. Unbreakable," he said with a serious look on his face.

That was certainly interesting. I have broken so many glass cups that it's not a big deal anymore; I just clean up the mess. I am quite an expert at looking for miniscule shrapnel by shining an electric torchlight on the floor. I am a professional at cleaning up the broken glass of cups and mugs. I can even redirect a glass cup that slipped out of my hand directly into the sink in mid-flight so it can explode without a large clean up.

"But unbreakable glass cups? This is a game changer," I thought.

"Let me demonstrate it to you, sir," the shopkeeper said."*Aaap dekho* (please watch)," he requested my attention.

And to my amazement, he dropped a glass on the floor. It hit the carpeted floor. It did not break at all.

"Wow, these Italians are good," I thought.

"This is real glass, not plastic, sir," the shopkeeper said, tapping the unbreakable glass.

I could not believe it. This is what I really wanted. What I really needed. My family in India would love this. Especially if they knew how many glass cups I had broken when no one was looking.

"How much is it?" I asked, acting as if I was not interested. If you act interested, they may jack up the price.

"Just $27 for a set of nine. Breakable glass cups are $20," he said.

This was the greatest deal of my life. At the rate at which I broke breakable glass cups, this would save me thousands of dollars in return.

"Deal. Get two sets of nine packed," I said.

One set for me for the rest of my life. One set to India for the rest of their lives.

I was so happy I had met this person who was going to change my life. No more cleaning up to do. No more glass shrapnel. I no longer had to use plastic cups like a kid.

I reached home and called my daughter to come down and witness the magic in action.

"Watch this," I said, opening the box full of unbreakable glass cups.

I took out one. I raised a glass cup with my hand, and threw it at the floor.

My daughter stood there in shock, certain I had turned crazy.

I have seen some folks throw coconuts at rocks to break them to please the Gods.

The unbreakable glass cups hit the tiled floor.

"*Ching,*" it sang.

And thousands of pieces of shrapnel were all over the floor. I wore a puzzled look on my face. My daughter looked even more puzzled.

"Why did you just do that?" she asked.

"It is unbreakable," I said slowly.

"What is unbreakable?" she asked in amazement.

I did not know what had just happened.

"Just do not mention this to your mother," I advised my daughter.

I can say for certain that the eight remaining unbreakable Italian glass cups broke in the next three months.

There is nothing that is unbreakable.

******

CHAPTER 68
MUSICAL CHAIRS

I hated Ammini, my mother-in-law, before my marriage to her daughter.

Ammini was the queen of musical chairs. She had topped the Musical Chair Competition at the church every year.

There was no way anyone else could compete with her family and win.

She had a devious tactic. She sped up when she was not in range of a chair, and kicked the potential winner out as soon as the music stopped.

She was way too competitive for the silly game of musical chairs. But winning for years on end had made her seriously competitive.

I saw this trait demonstrated at our church when my in-laws came to visit us.

During communion, our pew had gotten up and was waiting for the usher to let us into the queue.

From the corner of my eye, I spotted my mother-in-law getting up, leaving the pew from the opposite side, and heading directly to the priest.

She walked almost demurely, yet firmly. She went right to the front of the queue and cut-in at the first position, in true musical chair fashion. She looked up at the priest, ready to receive the communion.

Old habits die hard.

******

CHAPTER 69
HAMBURGER

"Here is a ten dollar bill. Please go to the fast-food joint and purchase a meal," I said to my dad in front of a McDonald's.

We were at the museum for the afternoon and I was trying to make my dad independent.

I wanted to see how he managed the language and the currency – my dad had been in the country visiting for a few months.

There were many people at the McDonald's. At least ten people were waiting in each line at the counter.

My dad took the money from me and walked towards the queue.

And then he did something strange.

He skipped to the head of a queue.

He took the ten-dollar bill and folded it lengthwise, in a v-shape.

He took the folded bill and placed it between the index and middle finger on his right hand.

He nudged the guy at the top of the line, moving him out of the queue with an elbow action.

My dad extended his right arm, with the v-shaped folded ten-dollar bill between his fingers.

He asked the person at the counter, "One hamburger, please."

It looked just as he would do in a crowded Indian shop, halfway around the world.

Do not assume anything.

******

CHAPTER 70
HEMI-SPHERE

"Be careful with the car," my friend Hemi's dad said. Hemi had just gotten his license and was taking his first trip alone in the car.

And he forgot to take his license with him.

It wasn't long before the cops stopped him.

"Please show me your license, sir," asked the officer.

Hemi started looking around. He saw a license lying on the seat next to him. When he handed it over to the police, he may not have noticed that it actually belonged to his dad.

Over the next few weeks Hemi's dad had to pay the fine and take a defensive driving class. The car insurance also took a hike.

For a ticket he never deserved.

Hemi's dad was certainly not a happy man that summer.

Carry your own license.

******

It was his stint at the convenience store that first brought Hemi close to death.

"Open the cash drawer and hand me all the money," the six-foot tall robber demanded – pointing a gun at the terrified Hemi.

And Hemi did, shivering in fear. He had sold about $300 worth of stuff that day.

"Get into that door," demanded the robber, pointing at the cold storage. Hemi got into the dark frozen room. He heard the robber close the door shut.

Hemi was soon shivering in the cold.

Hours passed. Hemi shivered more.

A customer who had found no one at the store counter called the police, and the police finally traced Hemi to the cold storage room.

When the door was opened, Hemi was shivering from both fear and cold.

The police tracked down the robber from the store surveillance video within weeks. The police found that the robber had used a fake gun to rob Hemi.

There is not much you can do about these things. Save yourself first.

******

It was the water scooter that brought Hemi close to death the second time.

It was springtime near the shore. And the water scooter looked so pretty; it was red and yellow.

"Red touch yellow, kill a fellow," Hemi remembered the old saying.

It was his first time on a water scooter.

The ride was so much fun. So much fun that he kept going.

Straight into the sea.

Far out into the sea.

It was getting late, so Hemi decided to head back home.

He turned the water scooter around.

And he turned the scooter around once more.

There was no land to be seen.

No home to go back to.

Hemi wanted to go west… east… north… south…

He watched the sun set. He watched the moon rise, and the stars follow.

He spotted Venus on one side.

It was getting dark.

The cold breeze seemed ready to lay him to his last sleep.

The red and yellow scooter and its tired rider went to sleep.

It got darker.

Hemi dreamed of his family that night – fondly, this time.

He thought of his friends, teachers and his dog.

And he went to sleep on a water scooter.

The water scooter bobbed around in the cold dark ocean.

With no particular direction to point to.

Water, water, everywhere.

It was midnight when the coast guard spotted the bright red-yellow scooter. They had been informed about someone missing.

"Anybody out there?" a voice shouted over the murmur of the boat. The light shone on Hemi's face.

Hemi thought he had reached heaven when he saw the bright light shining down on him. Literally. He was ready to meet the most Highest.

The waves splashing around the water scooter confused Hemi.

"Does heaven have water and water scooters?" he wondered.

"Thanks, Lord," he whispered.

The coast guard lowered the lights. Hemi came back to reality.

"Are you okay, sir?" the officer asked.

"Thank God," Hemi said, this time raising his eyes to the skies.

Know where you are going. Know how far you are going. Know your way back.

******

It was his work with a charity that brought Hemi to Atlanta, Georgia.

Hotwire gave him a cheap deal of $40 per day. Great hotel, it said.

Hemi felt uncomfortable checking into the Hotel Gaylord but he was too tired to find another place to stay.

After checking in, Hemi went to have lunch. When he came back to his room, it was totally empty.

Hemi's luggage – laptop, clothing, notes, everything – were gone.

He had nothing to wear for the next day.

Hemi left the room. He knocked on the neighbor's door. The door opened and Hemi saw two skinheads wearing earrings.

"Did you see anyone going into my room...?" he asked, trailing off. He took a step back.

"Not at all, do you want to come in?" asked one skinhead.

"No," said Hemi and ran downstairs to the lobby.

"Which is my room? Did I make a mistake? My room is empty!" Hemi screamed. The desk clerk handed him the phone and told him to call the police.

"I have been robbed," Hemi told the policewoman over the phone.

"Is it just a robbery? Have you or anyone you know been raped or murdered?" asked the officer.

"No I am alive. I just cannot find my clothes... I mean, laptop... I mean, notes... I mean, all my luggage is gone," Hemi stuttered into the phone.

"The Hotel Gaylord is in a high crime area. Unless there is someone murdered or raped, do not waste our time. Be careful where you take a room next time." The officer was curt, direct and matter-of-fact.

Hemi thanked the Gods that at least he had his wallet with him.

He left Hotel Gaylord immediately. He had to buy new clothes and pay for a new room – this time in a safer place.

Do not go for cheap, good-looking deals. You will end up paying for it. Trust your gut.

******

CHAPTER 71
CRYSTAL CLEAR

I loved the Lexus. It was a Hybrid.

It was silent like a baby. I mean, like a baby when the baby sleeps.

The dealership had exterior walls made up of rows of tall glass. It was spick and span, not a speck of dust on any pane.

The cappuccino machine was good. Free. I took a cup – it was a dull day and I was a bit sleepy.

They announced my name to pick up my new vehicle.

I saw my family waiting on the other side of the dealership.

I walked rather fast to join them.

I held a hot cup of cappuccino in my left hand. In the right was my cell phone.

There were several people in the lobby as I walked out as the proud owner of a new Lexus.

Suddenly my nose hit something. It hurt like hell. Then, I saw blood on the glass.

The cup of cappuccino had splashed all over the invisible glass. My cell phone was in pieces.

"Sir, are you okay?" the lady at the dealership asked.

"Kind of," I said, with blood streaking down my face.

I wondered why they kept the pane so neat that it was invisible.

"What happened?" my daughter asked when I reached them, "Can't you see where you are going?"

"Actually, I could see right through it," I said.

Some want to break the glass ceiling. I have no idea why. You do not even want to walk through a pane of glass.

******

CHAPTER 72
MIRACLE WHIP

Two of our projects had failed back-to-back. I had lost about a million dollars of effort because of a bad client who had sprouted green horns and a bad attitude. The board of directors did not care about the reasons. It wanted results.

I had nothing to go on. What I had made so far had turned out to be naught. I was disgusted at the greed and disappointed at the way human beings sometimes acted.

It was the second time in my life that I was up against everything with nothing to go on.

I believed that great things could happen out of nothing.

All I had to do was believe.

I went back to the drawing board.

I told the board that we would design a website that would change everything.

It was a bold statement to make, and a very hard one to keep.

This would be my last attempt. I would start with exactly nothing.

Still, I believed.

The last thing you can do is to not give up.

******

I wrote every line from scratch.

Three files. A spring night.

Those lines flowed from a hand – a hand calloused by the thousands of mistakes I had made in the past.

But it was an experienced hand that did not shake at all.

My hands wrote a poem. I gave it the name GAMI.

I was talking to Ji, a colleague, on the phone when I realized that we could make anything into GAMI. A strange name, that read IMAG-ine when read backwards.

I did imagine a weird Web from that moment on, and a way to see the Web like a spider.

We released the new site for our company, thinking it would bring us new business.

Little did I know that later, it would change us completely.

Little did I know I was starting a revolution with my fingers.

Tap, Tap, Tap; my imagination ran wild.

I entered worlds of dreams that no one had ever before seen.

Imagination routs reality.

******

I designed a way to organize, a new way to compute, and a totally new way to express and experience.

It was exciting. I showed it to a few people.

Each said they liked one thing or another.

Stash thought it looked cool. Ashok felt it could be something. Pradeep focused on a minor detail I didn't think would be significant.

Later, I thought that I should have taken his concern more seriously.

Twists and turns. And twists again. I was making clay that could be molded into anything.

It was magic, sheer magic.

Ritz named my creation ZCubes, after the Rubik's cube.

I named the template cube for my friend, Dan.

No name could say it all, but ZCubes could do it all.

We launched a company from a ranch in West Texas – in a horse stable.

So many people joined in. In weeks we did more than we had done in decades.

We had dreamt of doing wonderful things for so long, and now things were becoming crystals from nothing.

Like snowflakes out of cold air.

Imagine magic. It happens.

******

We had gone in the wrong direction before.

What we had before was fundamentally flawed.

We had followed a philosophy that just could never have solved it all.

A million dollars worth of effort had been vaporized by an irresponsible and dishonest client, and was not our fault.

When faced with deep adversity and utter despair, with nothing to hold on to, we created a simple website.

That website was a seedling that then transformed into something far bigger.

Far more than we could have ever even imagined.

Out of a string of bad luck, adversity, 'friends' turning into enemies, and failures.

We emerged with something of such value that we even could not have dreamt it.

When you believe, great things happen.

******

When you are in the right groove, things move blinding fast.

People joined us from all parts of the globe, resulting in a revolution in how information was seen and given.

Painters, singers, students, engineers, senior citizens, and children – everyone found something to do at ZCubes in the years that followed.

And we were not anywhere close to being done.

Hundreds of people may have chimed in the last two years.

Some came, to watch how it was turning out. Some got it. Others did not.

Jane. Jessica. Jay.

Maddy. Truly. Patil. Priya.

Hemi. Div. Span. Gops. Kish. Ash.

Dan. Maria. Amy. Ann.

Ritz. Ji. Jan.

Yi. Li. Manju. Raj. Sudhir. Divya. Const.

Jose. Celeste. Leon. John. Johnny. Mike.

Sunny. Sati. Umi. Fuzzy. Mahi. Das. Perry. Shwetz.

Varun. Mark. Kapil. Bart.

Rajen. Deep. Anee. Prash. Neenu.

Job. Kannax. Rashi. Sreej. Manjush.

Shalini. Preeti. Paru. Shome.

Kool. Bin. Dave. Geo. Geo.

Some I knew, many were new.

They were not just names.

They brought a passion that no one could match.

Loyalty. Dedication.

They were selfless, greedless, and driven.

We had launched a revolution that would last for years to come.

241

Revolutions are built on people – from ideas that are fundamental and entirely new.

Change comes when you least expect it.

******

Hundreds of thousands, maybe millions, more visitors kept coming to www.zcubes.com from all parts of the world, from nations I had not even seen.

It was hard to define what we were making.

Anand called it a canvas.

Rex said it might qualify to be a new generation of the Web; the third generation. It was December 2006 and John Markoff had coined the term "Web 3.0" just a month earlier in his landmark article in *The New York Times*.

Gerry Meyer quoted Wayne Gretzky at my keynote speech: "I skate to where the puck is going to be, not where it has been."

ZCubes, he pointed out, was where the puck was going to be. Some, like Desh, called it the future. Others, like Yurttas, called it brilliant.

I just called it magic.

Like snowflakes that sprang out of thin air.

Love adversity. Never give up.

******

CHAPTER 73
Y Z?

How did it happen?

It was what I could not see: a complete paradigm shift.

I had to work against myself.

I had to completely reorient my thoughts.

I had made enough mistakes to not make one more.

I had enemies to hate and friends to support.

False starts. Poor endings.

In the worst weather, when things could not have been worse.

Against all odds.

A steady calloused hand powered by pure imagination.

There is no success without mistakes. There is no creation without imagination.

******

Every stroke became a master stroke.

A masterpiece began drawing itself.

When the time is right and ripe, you will not lose. You cannot lose. As long as you have firm strokes and sheer determination to win.

The best things happen in the worst moments. Cherish them.

******

Whatever I had invented before this point had turned out to be insignificant, irrelevant and immaterial.

The greatest things occur when you stop. Kick out everything. Start with a blank canvas.

Evolution happens from the knowledge you have.

Revolutions are possible only when you start from absolutely nothing.

Nothing, that is, except your own creativity and an empty canvas.

Think irrational thoughts. Believe that it is possible to create things out of nothing, because it is possible.

******

CHAPTER 74
THE NEED TO
ADAPT

I called a press conference with reporters from all over the state to announce the impending release of our new software in India.

I was early to the press conference room. The conference started at 1:00 pm sharp.

I walked to the presenter's table.

I opened my laptop with the presentation.

I attached the power cord and then I looked for the power outlet.

The power outlet looked very different from what I was used to. The sockets did not match the plug.

I had lost the converter to local outlets.

"Do any of you have a convertor?" I asked.

There was no response.

I reduced the presentation to 15 minutes instead of an hour – the power on my computer ran out very quickly.

Get a universal adapter and carry it with your electronics. You never know which country you will find yourself in.

******

CHAPTER 75
GUIDE LINE

It is a father's duty to teach his children how to drive, and so I was eager to give my daughter her wings – her wheels.

I quickly realized that she knew nothing about driving, nothing whatsoever. She had never paid attention to how I drove. She thought it was none of her business to drive.

I guess that is something every parent has to go through.

I finally got her to drive in circles in her school parking lot.

It was her first turn to drive through the stop sign. She followed my instructions on how to stop, look to both sides, and then proceed.

The second time we came to the stop sign, I asked her to stop. Look. Then go.

She did.

The third time, she remembered the procedure herself.

The fourth time, she just went through the stop sign without pausing at all.

"What are you doing?" I screamed. "Why did you not stop at the stop sign?"

"I stopped the last time, did I not?" she retorted, just like a teenager. "Why do I have to stop every time, oh my God?"

Like... this is exactly why laws sound... like... stupid when you read them. They are written like... to include teenagers, duh!

******

CHAPTER 76
MULTI-MILLIONAIRE

There are many ways to become a millionaire, one of which is to work hard.

The other is to use my bank.

I deposited a small amount of money the other day.

The lady entered my account number as the amount.

I was instantly richer by about $10 million.

Strange things happen when you get a lot of money.

It is best if you are outside a car so you can jump up and down.

I thought of all the great things I could do that day.

Help poor people.

Establish a trust that takes care of the mentally ill.

You can do a lot of nice things with $10 million.

I voted against giving it to my children since they would turn irresponsible at a younger age.

Then I thought of going back and telling the bank official. I voted against that because the bank teller could possibly lose her job.

And I certainly did not want her to lose her job.

I went to have a Starbucks coffee to mull over this strange situation.

It is not every day that you get $10 million dollars to do whatever you would like to do.

After hours of deliberation, I decided to give it back.

I finally drove to the bank and found the teller and told her about the $10 million she had given me by mistake.

She apologized to me, which I said was totally

unnecessary, though she insisted on correcting the amount in spite of my being honest.

Honesty is generally the best policy, unless somebody may be killed because of your honesty. In which case, just shut up.

******

CHAPTER 77
BUNDLE OF JOY

I do not know what made me walk through those doors that Saturday morning.

Maybe it was the only thing to do on an otherwise ordinary day.

But that was the day I met her for the first time.

She had such kind brown eyes and black hair.

I could not forget her face.

******

"She sleeps most of the time," the lady said.

"She is adorable," I heard someone behind me say.

Everyone seemed to like her.

She ran around like any other kid and then she slept it off like a baby.

******

There were at least thirty pets at the Houston Humane Society shelter. "I liked a black lab," said my daughter, when she had finished looking at all the dogs up for adoption.

"I liked the one with the brown eyes and black fur," said my son, when he got back from browsing.

Both of them had picked a black lab with brown eyes.

Both had picked Dolly; the same Dolly I had wanted to adopt.

When you meet the one for you, you know.

******

"I'll clean her up," offered my daughter.

"I'll feed it so well it becomes fat enough to be two cats," offered my son.

"I hate cats. But that's beside the point," said my daughter, supporting my son.

"I'll take Dolly for a walk every day which will also be good daily exercise for me," I added.

Now that was an argument any spouse would accept.

The deal was made. We were going to adopt a pet.

******

The shelter released Dolly to us within a few days, after all the necessary vaccinations and other procedures. The paperwork was more than I had expected.

The trip to bring the Dolly home was rough. I did not know how to handle a dog in a fast-moving car.

Dolly jumped all over inside my wife's neat car. Licked the spotless windowpanes and the shiny door handles. Scratched the beige leather seats. Started biting the clean gear handle and the clear GPS screens.

"We need to take this car in for cleaning after this," I said reluctantly.

And then Dolly licked me, right on the lips.

I had no idea what to do with this puppy.

******

Back at home it got worse. We tied the new arrival to a door. She kept squealing.

I quickly assembled a newly purchased cage to put her in. I pulled her into the cage, and locked her up. I looked at this new addition to the family like she was some extraterrestrial being.

Dolly kept squealing. Whining. Barking. She certainly did not like the cage and she pulled at the bars, and tried to kick open the door.

"Bow... Wow... Bow..." Dolly kept complaining.

And off I went to office.

******

My phone rang.

"Dolly got out of her cage." My wife was very concerned. "Luckily the maid was here. She caught her and put her back into the cage. I am not sure what to do after the maid is gone."

This was getting more complicated. It looked like it may not work out after all.

Life is not perfect. Good things may not all look perfect.

******

My phone rang that evening while I was still at work.

"I like this dog," my wife said. "It escaped again from the cage, and started walking beside me. It seems to be a pleasant dog."

I breathed a sigh of relief.

Over the next few weeks, Dolly grew into a part of our family. Just like a newborn.

I taught Dolly a few commands.

Sit.

Stay.

Up.

Down.

Love.

The last command was special.

"Love," I would command.

And she would wag her tail fast, pull her ears back, and come up and lick all over your face.

255

A dog can teach you more about love than most other humans can. Get one.

******

CHAPTER 78
GOODBYE

It was 3 am. Calls at that time generally mean bad news.

My mother had passed away. Folks had thought she would somehow pull through this time as she invariably had many times before.

This time was different.

It was over.

I tried to remember as far back as I could.

A young woman with a beautiful face, who would dress me up, put talcum powder on my face, make my lunch, and beat the living daylights out of me for my many mistakes.

A slightly older woman with a slightly fatter face that wanted to give me the very best.

A middle aged-woman with a slightly wrinkled face that wanted to possess me and control me.

An older woman with a haggard face who wanted to fight me, defeat me and destroy me.

A much older woman, shriveled, thin and frail, who wanted to depend on me.

A silent old woman who was weak and hardly able to walk, and who wanted to hold on to me.

A woman, so short and frail that I could carry her with one arm – now silently had passed on to wait in another world for the rest of us to join her.

Many of us cried when she was dead. I cried out of joy that she had become what I wanted her to become. She was on to wherever she was going to, without dishonor and disgrace.

An innocent girl she had become from a possessed mind.

She had looked and acted a tenth of her age.

Like a sleeping baby, she now was silent.

******

She slept with flowers on her hair.

I had brought jasmine flowers. They looked like a garland of pearls around her face.

She wore a slight smile on her motionless lips.

She would not open her eyes again, but she kept talking to me with her silence.

Many people came; some I had forgotten, some I wanted to forget, and some I wanted to hate.

But this was her day. I was unimportant.

258

None of those she thought were her friends came.

Everyone who she had thought was not with her was there.

Young kids I had known had grown older; they now ran the world.

Kids my mother had kissed had children of their own now.

It could have been so much different.

It was not meant to be.

******

I thanked God that He had kept her alive to transform – to be born again – as a baby in body, mind and spirit.

A few months ago, she had tried to talk to me. Her words did not come out. With her weak hands and tired eyes she had mimed that God had seen everything.

"God, please protect me," she would say – those were the only words she could say. We heard her repeat them all the time.

I wished she could say more, but I was also not sure if I really wanted her to.

******

Right before her death, she was a baby in my arms.

Life had turned full circle.

It was time to let her go on a journey to a faraway place, beyond the stars – to a place that our eyes could not see.

******

Someone handed me a white handkerchief. It was to be placed on her face, to give her the last kiss.

I laid it on her face.

I went to her feet. I kneeled and kissed her feet.

For walking so far for me.

For carrying me for years when I could not walk.

I went to her tummy. I kneeled and kissed her tummy.

For carrying me for months in her womb – my home before I was born.

For feeding me for years after I was born.

I went to her face. I kneeled and kissed her forehead.

For giving me talent, wisdom and intelligence to do truly incredible things.

For guiding me when I was gullible. For hating me when I was not.

For making promises I had decided to keep.

For breaking promises she had said she would keep.

For showing me sights that I would have missed.

For being my eyes, ears and lips — when I could not see, hear or say.

For being my self, until I had one myself.

I had forgotten to kiss her goodbye.

So I kneeled and kissed her face through the white handkerchief.

The Jasmine flowers framed her face.

It felt like kissing a cold stone this time.

******

They lowered her to her final resting place.

I threw in a fistful of mud. I was darn happy to see her go the way she did, and even though my eyes were full of tears, my heart was full of joy.

The crowd dissolved quickly.

She would be alone from tonight on.

I wasn't sure if she would make it to heaven, but if babies died and went there, she stood a hell of a chance.

All mistakes must be forgiven. None should be forgotten.

******

CHAPTER 79
FAMILYSHIP

You are born into a family. Familyship is granted to you by default, like citizenship. There is no chance to get rid of it if you do not like it.

It is like your race or your face; you cannot change it, forever.

Unless you are Michael Jackson.

******

You cannot change where you are from. But you can change where you are going.

You cannot change who your parents are. But you can change who your friends are.

Love your family.

******

Relationships start, but generally never end. They only vary in quality over time and varying circumstances.

A relationship can start with a person whom you have just heard about.

262

You never even need to meet.

Until both forget each other, a relationship exists.

******

CHAPTER 80
A HUMERUS STORY

"Dad, come with me to our school playground, I want to show you a new trick," my son said.

He showed off his skills on the monkey bars. Dolly and I watched in amazement the new tricks my son had to show us.

Then I saw the red soccer ball, left in the field from a past game.

For the next six months, that ball changed my life.

******

I loved soccer. I was a notorious defender who could slice people in two on the field.

I never cared about the ball; instead, I generally watched the person running after the ball. That was the one I would tackle.

I loved soccer so much that even after twenty years I wanted to play the game right away.

My son, Dolly and I ran to the soccer field.

******

I started showing my son a few tricks of the game.

I have always been disappointed seeing other fathers teach their kids baseball or basketball, because I had no clue about either.

******

I had been to a baseball match at Enron field, the Astros versus the Yankees.

I could not see the ball or follow the game.

There seemed to be no real rules. Suddenly the viewers would applaud and scream at a good shot. The music would pick up. A train would move.

People lined up at stalls to buy popcorn, hotdogs and huge liter-size Coke cups.

I just could never track the ball. It was too small and too fast to be seen.

It looked like they needed a brighter, bigger and shiny ball.

******

I loved watching basketball. I admired Air Jordan. The Rockets. The Spurs.

But I did not really know enough to teach my kids about that game.

In soccer, though, I knew a thing or two. It was my second best game.

******

I kicked the red ball. It rose in the air and landed several yards away. I knew my legs still had it.

I had tied Dolly's leash around my arm so that I could control her better.

She started running after the ball. Maybe she also wanted to play soccer.

Did dogs like soccer? Did it come naturally to them?

I wanted to find out.

******

This time I kicked the ball really hard. It went flying into the air.

266

My son said he felt proud of me.

And Dolly felt proud of me too, because she watched the ball and started running after the ball.

I ran with her.

Puppies run real fast. Dolly ran faster. She was a born dasher.

I could run fast too.

Dolly and I went up the field to fetch the bright red ball.

Faster and faster. I could run like a gazelle. My legs ran faster than my head.

Dolly got ahead of me.

I got ahead of her.

The ball started its descent.

It landed just ahead of us.

I knew I could kick it again, just ahead of Dolly.

But Dolly was faster. She was ahead of me ever so slightly.

And she seemed to have a better lead.

With a leap, she pounced on the ball.

I was just behind her now.

She had caught the ball.

Score: Dolly One, Me Zero.

When a dog catches a ball, it stops. Dogs do not kick the ball further like humans do.

She pounced on the ball and stopped instantly, like all retrievers do.

******

I remembered Newton's first law.

Nothing else was ahead of me except the bright red ball. But Dolly stood over the ball, looking proudly back into my eyes. Frozen in time. She had beaten me.

I knew there was no escape. I was heading towards them like a freight train.

I jumped above the ball and Dolly just in time, hoping to miss both of them, but I still hit them.

I was airborne. Like Superman, again without the cape on my back and the curl on my forehead.

Flying without the powers.

******

I landed on my left arm and lost all sensation in it instantly.

In just one moment it felt like my arm was just a dead weight on my shoulder.

My face hit the ground next.

Thud. It was hard.

My left arm no longer moved.

It was a funny feeling. Going from two-armed to one-armed in an instant is a defining moment.

******

With my other and only usable arm, I fished out my cell phone.

9-1-1.

The eagle had landed. One wing was out.

The ride to the hospital was quiet.

Why did I have to kick a soccer ball? Why did I have to race a puppy?

You do not need to. But that is what family is all about.

******

"X-Rays show that your arm is completely fractured. Your humerus is in two pieces," said the doctor.

"You will certainly need surgery," said a worried nurse.

"You will be in a cast for four to six months," said the doctor.

"Finally, I can take a break," I thought. It was my first vacation since I had invented magic itself. I certainly needed one.

Every dark cloud has a silver lining. Look for it.

******

CHAPTER 81
POINT... SHOOT...

I loved taking pictures.

The best pictures required a sophisticated camera.

Now that I had only one arm for six months, I decided it was time to take up photography.

My friend Dan gave me his Canon Rebel XT.

It was a top-of-the-line camera with a variety of lenses that made no sense to me.

I tried to take a picture.

Click.

Nothing happened. Oops, I had not switched it on. I switched it on.

Click.

Nothing happened.

"This must be some sophisticated camera," I said to myself. "I can't even turn it on."

I decided to go back to electronics that I could operate, like my laptop.

A week later, I got the manual for the camera.

I read it from front to back.

I switched on the camera, just like the manual said.

Click.

Nothing happened.

I gave up photography this time. This was too complex for me.

If I could not even start the device, it was time to give up without telling anyone else about it.

So I did.

I had determined by now that I would never be good at photography.

For months, I left it and did normal things like watching *Hannity and Colmes*, a reflection of how unfair the world actually is.

******

Months later, I felt like giving it another shot. It had become a challenge.

I had read the manual. I had followed the instructions. And the camera had not clicked.

Maybe it was a sophisticated catch mechanism?

Fuzzy logic?

Artificial Intelligence?

"Dad, did you check if there is a battery in the camera?" asked my son.

Actually, the battery had not been placed inside the camera.

Check all the basics first. I mean, the really basic things.

******

CHAPTER 82
LOVE THY ENEMY

"Love Thy Enemies," Jesus said, the Bible says.

There is nothing more difficult to do.

Enemies are the secret to your survival; without enemies, life is a dull period of existence.

Without opposition, your muscles weaken.

It is easy to love your friends, but there is nothing great about loving lovable people.

Loving your enemies is a thousand times greater and tougher than loving a friend.

******

Your best enemies are the best friends you can have.

Your best friends are the worst enemies you can have.

An enemy pushes you harder.

A friend makes you feel good.

A friend is useful, but an enemy is a necessity.

******

To those who try to harm, hurt, trick, and inveigle you – treat them with respect, consideration and deference.

Keep a watchful eye, but without anger. Do not waste time hating them.

Instead, channel your anger to your advantage.

The best way to hurt an enemy is to be thousands of times more successful than they would ever want you to be.

Always, you must treat an enemy with kindness. There is a good reason for it.

Without enemies, you cannot think hard enough.

They will drive you crazy, drive you mad and drive you to heights you could never imagine.

An easy life is not worth it.

A diamond has to be cut to make it shine.

A stone has to roll over and over – thousands of times – to become smooth.

Love does not make you shiny and smooth. Hate does.

******

I was at a gas station the other day when I witnessed a strange exchange.

A man was screaming at another.

The second man had been taking longer than expected to pump gas into his car. Words got nasty and deteriorated into four letter words.

The second man kept smiling as if he were not affected by anything the first man said. This made the first man angrier.

Finally the second man finished with filling up his car. While getting into the car, he said, "Jesus loves you too."

It sounded strange, to hear something like that said to a cursing stranger. I wasn't sure what he meant. Was it sarcasm? Was he really serious?

Then I remembered the words, "Love Thy Enemies."

I had just seen it in practice between two strangers who would forever remain strangers.

For some reason, one had shown hate.

The other had chosen to show love.

It is my choice.

******

```
        *
       * *
      * * *
     * * * *
    * * * * *
   * * * * * *
```

Seek. Learn. Look.

And make lots of mistakes.


```
   * * * * * *
```


Be greedless, fearless and selfless.

Just enjoy life!


```
   * * * * * *
    * * * * *
     * * * *
      * * *
       * *
        *
```